A Scenic Route through the Old Testament

A Scenic Route through the Old Testament

Alec Motyer

Inter-Varsity Press

INTER-VARSITY PRESS
38 De Montfort Street, Leicester LE1 7GP, UK

British Library Cataloguing-in-Publication Data
A catalogue record for this book is available from the British
Library.

ISBN 0–85111–152–1

Set in Linotron Baskerville

Photoset by Parker Typesetting Service, Leicester

Printed and bound in Great Britain
by Cox & Wyman Ltd, Reading, Berkshire

*Inter-Varsity Press is the book-publishing division of the Universities and
Colleges Christian Fellowship (formerly the Inter-Varsity Fellowship), a
student movement linking Christian Unions in universities and colleges
throughout the United Kingdom and the Republic of Ireland, and a
member movement of the International Fellowship of Evangelical
Students. For information about local and national activities write to
UCCF, 38 De Montfort Street, Leicester LE1 7GP*

Contents

Preface

In the first half of 1989, while I was Vicar of Christ Church Westbourne, the Adult Education Committee of the Bournemouth Deanery (the local grouping of Church of England churches) invited me to give a series of lectures on the Old Testament. I owe a big debt of gratitude to Keith Rawlings who 'fathered' the enterprise, and to the resolute company who braved winter nights and made the whole series so memorable and happy for me.

This was the early proving ground for five of the six chapters of this book, with their associated schemes of Bible reading. I have now added the chapter and readings on wisdom for the sake of completeness.

As I see it, the scheme of readings and notes is much more important than the introductory chapters. The Bible is just what the advertisers claim for Bisto gravy – as soon as the aroma wafts their way, the Bisto kids lift their noses to it and head for home! When we settle down to reading the Bible we soon catch the scent, and the Bible's Lord himself will be our teacher.

This is not to say that the chapters are unimportant. It is in them that the panorama of the Old Testament scene is spread out. They are meant to be lookout points. Read them with Bible in hand and look up the references that are given. But should you find them unduly hard going, get on with the readings and return to the chapters later.

May the Lord richly bless you as you come with me for a country walk through the first and larger part of his word!

Alec Motyer
Bishopsteignton, Devon

Introduction

A little while ago I stood beside the Pyramids at Gizeh and looked out into the Egyptian desert. Until that moment I had not properly realized just how sandy, barren and trackless it is. Somewhere out there an oasis would await the traveller, but only after hours, even days, of weary toil.

Do you feel that way about the Old Testament? Don't be embarrassed about it, many people do, and no wonder! For not only is it a large book, but it also seems remote from our modern needs and ways, 'an antique land', pretty profitless, hard to find your way about.

But the oases are there too! Sunday School and other early memories tell us of pretty good stories about Samson, Samuel and David; Christmas services have given us a nodding acquaintance with bits about a child being born; Handel's Messiah has even made parts of the Old Testament distinctly singable. But the occasional oasis does not change the desert, does it?

The Old Testament is not really like that at all! Far from being a desert, it is actually a rather spectacular countryside. So come with me, not on a demanding safari, but on an enjoyable walk from one scenic viewpoint to another.

Much of the Old Testament consists of history books, so we will thread our way through the stories to meet the people and find out what they are saying to us. The Old Testament is also 'Law'. Don't let the word scare you for it really means 'teaching', God's authoritative and loving teaching about what is true and how to live: the actual down-to-earth instruction and direction we need. And there is prophecy, religion, worship and wisdom, but above all and through it all there is the revelation of God.

We are going to look at these topics in turn. In each case I have written an introductory guide, to give an overall view, to set the scene, and then each introduction is followed by four weeks of daily readings with brief notes. These are not set out in the order they come in the Bible, but are chosen to illustrate the theme in question.

Scenery speaks to us. Whether it is beautiful or awesome, tranquil or turbulent, it is saying something about its Creator. Just so, we will find that our scenic route through the Old Testament is constantly addressing us. In this way it is our privilege to stand alongside our Lord Jesus Christ. For him, the Old Testament was the word of God and every aspect of it bore witness to him (Luke 24:44; John 5:31). It is the same for us: this ancient word of God leaps across the centuries to tell us about Jesus and how we are to live for him.

In the Old Testament the past speaks to the present.

1

The Voice of History

A review

Between the time when the Lord called Abraham (Genesis 12) and the time of Malachi, the last of the prophets, there is about 1500 years. Within this time span the Old Testament tells how the Lord chose one man, gave him a family and made the family a nation. Patiently he persevered with that nation through thick and thin, never deviating from his freely-given commitment to be their God.

This is what the story outline looks like:

Topic	References	Dates
The Family: Abraham Isaac Jacob and his twelve sons	Genesis Genesis 12 – 25 Genesis 21 – 35 Genesis 25 – 50	2000–1500 BC
The Nation: Moses and the Exodus Joshua and the Conquest Early life in Canaan	Exodus – Ruth Exodus – Deuteronomy Joshua Judges, Ruth	1400–1100 BC
The Monarchy: The first king: Saul David Solomon	 1 Samuel 1 Samuel 16 – 1 Kings 2 1 Chronicles 10 – 29 1 Kings 1 – 11 2 Chronicles 1 – 9	1100–586 BC 1050–1000 BC 1000–960 960–930
The Two Kingdoms: The Kings of Judah The Kings of Israel	1 Kings 12 1 Kings 12 – 2 Kings 25 2 Chronicles 10 – 36 1 Kings 12 – 2 Kings 17	 930–586 BC 930–722 BC
The Exile: Babylon	2 Kings 25	586–540 BC
The Return	Ezra, Nehemiah	539 BC

A chart can only give an impression: this is what the 'skeleton' of Old Testament history looks like. But put some flesh on the bare bones by following the events through on the map.

One man to bless the world

God had a worldwide purpose when he called Abram from Ur of the Chaldees (Genesis 11:31 – 12:5; 15:7) and we, marvelling at the simple trust of the man who 'went, even though he did not know where he was going' (Hebrews 11:8), can follow him along the established trade route from Ur to Haran and on into Canaan. He went on his way trusting the promises God had made to him – that he would be a universal blessing (Genesis 12:2,3) and possess the land of Canaan (Genesis 15:7). In due course the promises passed to Isaac (Genesis 17:19–21), then to Jacob (Genesis 27:27–29; 28:13–15).

Possessing the land

Part of the promise was fulfilled when Jacob's sons, now a large nation (Exodus 1:1–7), left Egypt under Moses and later entered and possessed Canaan under Joshua. The book of Joshua (see Joshua 1:1–5; 21:43–45) tells how the land was conquered. Judges chapter 1 sketches how individual tribes claimed their inheritance, but the main message of Judges is of the good care of the Lord in providing judge-deliverers according to the people's need, but contrary to their deserving (Judges 2:10–19).

The kings

Then they asked for a king (1 Samuel 8:6) and, after the failure of Saul's kingship (1 Samuel 8:1–7; 10:20–24; 13:13,14; 15:26), David united the kingdom round his new capital city, Jerusalem (2 Samuel 5:6–9). His son Solomon further cemented this unity by building in Jerusalem a temple or dwelling-place for the Lord (1 Kings 6:1, 37–38).

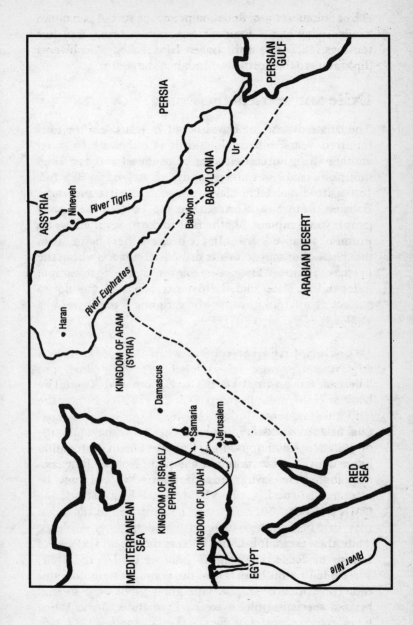

13

But Solomon's son, Rehoboam, was the sort of person we would today call a 'loser'. The kingdom broke into two (1 Kings 12:1–19) with Israel (also called 'Jacob' and 'Ephraim') to the north, and Judah to the south.

Exile and return

The single dynasty of David lasted in Jerusalem for four hundred years, but in the north one dynasty followed another. King succeeded king by conquest and assassination until Israel was taken captive to Assyria in 722 BC. Judah, however, did not fall to Assyria's imperial successor, Babylon, until 586 BC and then the exile of the Lord's people was complete. But the faithful Lord never allows his promises to lapse (Ezra 1:1). He brought them home again in 539 BC, but only to live as provincial subjects within the Persian Empire. They were never again a sovereign, independent state, and the dynasty of David was not to surface again until he came whose right it is to reign (Luke 1:29–33).

What sort of history?

There are five things we can say about Old Testament history.

Old Testament history is reliable
Specialist opinion regarding Old Testament history has undergone a wide pendulum swing. Not so long ago specialists were saying that the stories should only be accepted as true if verified by evidence from outside the Old Testament. But now many are prepared to allow that they can be assumed to be true unless other evidence contradicts them. It is fair to say that the major tendency of outside evidence is to confirm what we read in the Bible. But we have a much surer foundation to rest on than this piece of evidence or that. Our great privilege is to look beyond specialist opinion to the Lord Jesus Christ. When he referred to stories in the Old Testament, it is plain that

he accepted them as the wholly reliable word of God, and we who follow him need have no hesitation in accepting as true whatever the Old Testament is found to affirm about events and their sequence.

The words 'found to affirm' are important. Old Testament history is not problem-free. It is not easy, for example, to 'fit together' the reigns of the kings of Israel and Judah from dates and chronologies supplied by the books of Kings; neither is it certain who is referred to as 'Darius the Mede' in Daniel 5:31. On the other hand it is clear from archaeology that the stories of Abraham, Isaac, Jacob and Joseph accurately reflect life and customs in the period 2000–1500 BC. Details (like the very existence of Belshazzar, Daniel 5), formerly disputed, are now well established. We need to work at the stories until we are sure what it is the Old Testament is saying and claiming.

Old Testament history is selective

In this it is no different from every attempt to write history. Not even the longest history book, inside or outside the Bible, contains all that happened in its chosen period. H.A.L. Fisher wrote his *History of Europe* without making any reference to my grandmother. The same is true of R. F. Foster in his book *Modern Ireland 1600–1972*, even though the old lady lived in Ireland well within this period. Were I to write of the years 1850–1939, Grandma would figure very largely indeed. It is all a matter of what a writer thinks important.

Even historians who cannot discern any purpose in the flow of history still have to decide what to include and what to leave out. This is just as true of the Old Testament, not because it contains a peculiar sort of history, or because its writers were ignorant or biased, but because selection is the only way to write history.

Take Manasseh as an example. He reigned for many years over Judah (690–640 BC) and economically, politically and militarily he was an astute ruler, but 2 Kings tells us nothing of all this. Only eighteen verses are allotted to his fifty-five years (2 Kings 21:1–18) and they say, in effect, only one thing about Manasseh: 'He did evil in the eyes of the Lord' (verse 2).

Fifty-five years and only one fact! It would be easy to dismiss such history writing as not history at all. How very different it is from modern histories with their social, economic, political and military detail! But notice verse 17:

> . . . the other events of Manasseh's reign . . . all
> that he did . . . are they not written in the books of
> the annals of the kings of Judah?

In other words, the Old Testament historian had all the facts available, but he simply did not think them important for his purpose. Rather, this was his concern:

> Nevertheless the Lord did not turn away from the
> heat of his fierce anger . . . against Judah because
> of all that Manasseh had done . . . So the Lord
> said: 'I will remove Judah . . . I will reject
> Jerusalem . . .' (2 Kings 23:26,27).

The point is that it was Manasseh's moral and spiritual failure that subsequently caused the ruin of Judah and Jerusalem. In 2 Kings 23:26 notice the word 'nevertheless'. Manasseh was succeeded by Josiah (2 Kings 22 – 23). Unlike his father he was devoted to the Lord. Indeed, of all the kings of Judah he came nearest to the ideal, the 'golden boy' David. Think of it this way: Manasseh dropped a huge brick into the pond; Josiah, by his godliness and his reforms, fetched the brick out again, but nothing could stop the ripples that Manasseh had set in motion.

Why then should we need to know of Manasseh's domestic and foreign policies? It was not on them that history turned, for it is righteousness, not astuteness, that exalts a nation (Proverbs 14:34). All Old Testament history is selectively written to demonstrate this single principle. The fortunes of nations are settled not by economic, political, military or diplomatic factors, but by their standing before God.

Old Testament history is God-centred

The Hebrew Bible – the 'Old Testament' – consists of three sections. They are arranged differently from our English versions (which follow the order given in the 'Septuagint', the Greek translation of the Old Testament), and look like this:

The Law:
  Genesis, Exodus, Leviticus, Numbers, Deuteronomy

The Prophets:
  (a) The Former Prophets:
      Joshua, Judges, Samuel, Kings.

  (b) The Latter Prophets:
      Isaiah, Jeremiah, Ezekiel.
      Hosea, Joel, Amos, Obadiah, Jonah, Micah,
      Nahum, Habakkuk, Zephaniah, Haggai,
      Zechariah, Malachi.

The Writings:
  Psalms, Job, Proverbs.
  Song of Songs, Ruth, Lamentations, Ecclesiastes,
  Esther.
  Daniel, Ezra, Nehemiah, Chronicles.

This is the Bible as Jesus knew it. In the Upper Room on the first Easter Day he spoke to his disciples about how 'everything must be fulfilled that is written about me in the Law of Moses, the Prophets and the Psalms' (Luke 24:44). It is pretty marvellous to realize that we have the same Bible the Lord Jesus knew and loved.

But the particular point to notice is that the early editors, who organized the Bible books into the three-section order of the Hebrew Bible, described the history books of Samuel and Kings as 'prophets'. How can this be? What does it mean?

When we speak of 'prophets' we often mean 'predicters' or 'forecasters', but this is only one of the things a prophet did. Acts 2:11 and 17 will help us here. As the crowd listened to the apostles speaking on the Day of Pentecost, Peter reminded them that Joel had predicted 'your sons and daughters will prophesy'. However, what the listeners heard them saying was not prediction but 'the wonders of God'. This is how the Old Testament history books are 'prophecy': they are written in order to tell us about God and the way he runs the world; they are a record of his wonderful works.

Listen to Amos:

> Did I not bring Israel up from Egypt, the
> Philistines from Caphtor and the Arameans
> from Kir? (Amos 9:7).

This must have been a shock to Amos' listeners. They had been brought up to believe that their God's 'wonderful works' in bringing them out from Egyptian slavery were unique to them. This was right as far as it went. Sadly, however, they had come to think of the exodus simply as a date on the calendar, and of themselves as right with God simply because that date had passed. It was like the song which still goes the rounds at Christmas time, 'Man shall live for evermore because of Christmas Day'. In one sense nothing could be more true, for Jesus came to save and does save all who trust him. But in another sense nothing could be more false or misleading, because the mere fact of Christmas as a date on the calendar saves no-one.

So Amos was challenging a deadly spiritual complacency which said 'we must be right with God because the exodus happened', irrespective of personal trust or obedience or holiness. He challenged it head on: 'As far as the exodus is concerned, why, you are no different from anyone else! Who do you think masterminded the migration of the Philistines from Caphtor and of the Arameans from Kir? You boast of your exodus but your God is so great that he is behind every movement of peoples and nations!' He is the God of *all* history!

Or listen to Isaiah:
> Woe to the Assyrian, the rod of my anger,
> in whose hand is the club of my wrath!
> I send him against a godless nation . . .
> to seize loot and snatch plunder . . .
> But this is not what he intends . . .
> his purpose is to destroy,
> to put an end to many nations . . .
>
> I will punish the king of Assyria for the wilful
> pride of his heart . . .
>
> Does the axe raise itself above him who swings it,
> or the saw boast against him who uses it?
> (Isaiah 10:5–15).

Assyria was the superpower of the day. We must not belittle that power simply because their weapons seem so primitive compared with the savage weapons of destruction which are the childish pride of nations today. The Assyrians had developed the most advanced war machine of their time; they were dreaded for a seemingly invincible capacity for total war. But, says Isaiah, what is Assyria but an expression of the Lord's wrath (verse 5), a messenger on the Lord's errand (verse 6) and a tool in the Lord's hand (verse 15)? The superpower on earth and the superior power of a sovereign God!

One major lesson of all the history books, and one reason why so much of the Old Testament is occupied with history, is that we may see that behind all events, and behind the whole sequence of events, there is a great and wonderful God engineering and controlling everything and working his purposes out in the flow of history.

Old Testament history is moral
Stay with Isaiah 10:5–15. Assyria invaded Judah and threatened Jerusalem in 701 BC. It was a justly deserved disaster for the Judahites and Assyria was the Lord's chastising rod. But from the point of view of the King of

Assyria nothing of the sort was happening. He was an imperialist. He took it for granted that it was his right to rule the world, that if he so wished he would jolly well do so, and Jerusalem was as helplessly and rightfully his prey as all the other nations he had conquered (verses 7–11). He was wholly motivated by what Isaiah calls his 'wilful pride' (verse 12). Under a sovereign God Assyria's power would be used for the Lord's holy purposes (verses 6,12); under a holy God Assyria's pride would be punished (verses 12–15).

The king of Assyria was both a tool in the Lord's hand and a responsible agent in his own right. Isaiah helps us to understand this a little by suggesting an illustration:

> Because your insolence has reached my ears, I will
> put . . . my bit in your mouth and I will make you
> return by the way you came (Isaiah 37:29).

The Assyrian king was like a powerful horse, with enormous energy and drive, but the Lord was the rider determining where and to what extent that power may be used. In this way the Bible reveals a God who is not only fully sovereign, but undeviatingly holy. It also reveals a world in which people are fully responsible for what they do and yet live within the control of divine rule.

Many are troubled by the fact that the Old Testament seems so full of war and cruelty: 'Such a savage book' people say.

There are three things to be said about this. First, we must be careful not to criticize the Old Testament for being *realistic*. Its history, after all, is about this world, and if it contained no wars with their cruelties, probably the same people who accuse it of savagery would be the first to criticize it for living in a dream world!

Secondly, the Old Testament does not necessarily approve of all it records. Its stories rarely embody a moral comment one way or the other; we are usually left to draw our own conclusions of right or wrong. Consequently, to be actually told in 2 Samuel 11:27 that 'the thing David had done displeased the Lord' is somewhat out of the ordinary.

Another incident in the life of David is allowed to pass without comment. The Lord brought David to the throne without his fighting for it. He promised it to David and kept his promises (2 Samuel 7:8–11). Equally, David, for his part, resolutely refused to seize the throne for himself (1 Samuel 24:4–7; 26:8–11). Once he was on the throne, however, what do we find? He went to war against the poor rump of Saul's kingdom ruled by the incompetent and rather pathetic Ishbosheth (2 Samuel 2:8 – 4:12). By doing so he sowed seeds of bloodshed that would in due course become a harvest of hatred and division.

Was this war justified? Should not David have continued to trust that the Lord who had kept his promises so far would go on keeping promises until they were all fulfilled? Does the Old Testament approve of this war-making? Surely not! It is recorded, not because the Old Testament delights in war, but because its people (even the best of them) are tragically human and their lives blighted by human frailties.

In other words, the history books of the Old Testament not only reveal God but also reveal people. Even the best of them were sinful – lustful, ambitious, cruel, mistaken. Like us, they failed, and their failures are faithfully recorded in this most honest of books. Indeed, isn't it one of the greatest of the 'wonders of God' that he continues to bother with such people?

Thirdly, the long sweep of Old Testament history allows us to see the holy God governing the world by his own moral laws. Joshua entered Canaan with a mandate which horrifies us: he was to put to death every human being without regard to age or sex (*e.g.* Joshua 6:21). But this frightfulness is the end of a long story which began in Genesis 15:16. The time was four hundred years earlier; the Lord was speaking to Abraham.

> In the fourth generation your descendants will come back here, for the sin of the Amorites has not yet reached its full measure.

Even on a timescale of centuries, history is governed by the Lord's moral rules. To take the land of the Amorites from them and give it to Abraham just like that would have been an injustice. They were its rightful owners and their rights had to be respected. But in four hundred years' time the story would be different. They would have had four centuries of probation and by the end of that time 'their iniquity' would have reached 'full measure'. Awful as would be their end, it was no more than the wages of their sin (Romans 6:23). 'Will not the Judge of all the earth do right?' (Genesis 18:25).

Old Testament history is a record of failure

The people asked for a king (1 Samuel 8:5; 12:12) because they thought that an organized monarchy would be the end of all their troubles. It would have been if only they were able to find a king equal to the task!

In the southern kingdom of Judah, the descendants of David sat on his throne in ordered succession. David was the Lord's own king; he and his sons sat on what is called 'the Lord's throne' (1 Chronicles 29:23). Yet their kingdom failed and, to the human eye, the dynasty petered out.

The northern kingdom of Israel was ruled by monarchs who came to the throne by natural gifts of leadership and in pursuit of personal ambition. Although one dynasty after another did the best that human ability could achieve, this kingdom, too, failed and disappeared.

In this way Old Testament history is one long cry for something better, for a true king who would satisfy his people's aspirations for peace and safety, reigning in perfection and ruling in righteousness. Like every other 'voice' in the Old Testament, the voice of history is a prayer for the coming of the Messiah.

**A Scenic Route Through
Old Testament History**

**Meet the leading figures of the Old Testament at
turning-points in the story of the people of God**

Four weeks of short daily Bible readings with brief notes

Week 1: Abraham, Isaac, Jacob and Joseph

*Day 1. Read Genesis 12:1–9. Walking with God: great
promises, partial obedience*

About 2000 years before Christ, the Lord chose and called
one man, Abram, intending to bless him and to make him a
blessing to others (verse 2), and ultimately to bless the
whole world through him. The rest of the story of the Bible
shows how God kept this promise. The Lord Jesus, born in
the line of Abraham, is the blessing the whole world needs.
Abram was told to leave his 'father's household' (verse 1),
but he took Lot (verse 5): we are never quite what we ought
to be! But the Lord continued to bother with him for all
that (verse 7).

*Day 2. Read Genesis 18:1–15; 21:1–7. Abraham's
family, a promise kept*

God is not limited by what we call impossible (18:11). He
promised a family to Abraham and a family he would have.
Nothing is too hard for the Lord (18:14). But it was not till
more than thirteen years later that the promise was kept.
They must have seemed long years to Abraham and his
wife – but what joy the faithfulness of God brought with it!
(21:6). Between chapters 18 and 21 we see something of
the greatness of Abraham (18:22–33) and something of his
weakness (20:1–2). God does not keep his promises to us
because of our worthiness, but simply because his love for
us is a faithful love.

Day 3. Read Genesis 22:1–18. A great test and a great faith

When human sacrifice was part of surrounding pagan religion, it is not surprising that the thought might have occurred to Abraham whether he loved his God sufficiently to make such a costly response. But when God thus tested him, he rose to the occasion. Verse 5 shows his faith: 'We will go, we will worship ... we will come back.' God had promised that the continuation of Abraham's family would be through Isaac; even if Isaac died on the altar the promises of God would not fail. Verse 13 shows how Abraham understood the meaning of the sacrifices he offered: the beast dying instead of the human.

Day 4. Read Genesis 26:1–13. Blessings abound

By now Abraham has died; Isaac has married Rebekah and they have twin sons, Esau and Jacob. Time passes; people come and go; God does not change. In a time of need he is at hand to re-affirm his protection and provision for his people (verses 1–3), and, notwithstanding the famine, Isaac reaps abundantly (verse 12). Not only so but the Lord also repeats to Isaac the great promises he had made to Abraham (verses 3–5). How odd, then, that Isaac should be afraid and practise deceit in order to make himself secure! (verse 7). How slow we are to learn to trust the Lord! How quick we are to turn to our own absurd safeguards! But, once more, the Lord does not change: he loves us because he loves us.

Day 5. Read Genesis 28:10–22. The promise is handed on again

In Isaac's old age, his sons Esau and Jacob fell out because of Jacob's extreme treachery to his brother. In consequence, Jacob had to leave home. Here we learn how inexplicable to our wisdom the purposes of God are: though Jacob was the younger of the twins, and though he turned out a person of dubious integrity, he was chosen before birth (25:23; Romans 9:10–12) to inherit God's promises to Abraham and the world (verses 13,14). In verse 20 note the telltale 'If' – the Lord has promised not to leave Jacob (verse 15), but Jacob is not yet a firm believer. But God loves to be trusted. The Lord Jesus made 'Jacob's ladder' a picture of himself as the way we come to God and God's blessings come to us (verse 12; John 1:51). To Jacob (as to us) it should have been a persuader to trust God fully.

Day 6. Read Genesis 32:1–31. When I am weak, then I am strong

Though Jacob prayed a wonderful prayer (verses 9–12), he did not trust God to answer it, for immediately he set out to win Isaac's favour by his own clever gifts. But he learned that when, in helpless agony with his hip out of joint, he sought blessing (verse 26), he became the man who 'overcame'.

Day 7. Read Genesis 50:1–20. The purposeful ups and downs of life

Much time had passed. Jacob and his large family have become resident aliens in Egypt where his son, Joseph, is prime minister. The story of Joseph is one of suffering: brotherly hatred, sold into slavery, wrongful accusation, years of imprisonment, disappointed hopes. All this we have had to skip over, but we meet Joseph as, at the end of his life, he looks back and teaches us how to interpret its ups and downs: 'God intended it' – it was all part of a divine purpose; 'God intended it for good' – a divine beneficial purpose (verse 20).

Week 2: Moses, Joshua and the Judges

Day 1. Read Exodus 2:1–9. The hidden hand of God

The Bible never tells us why the Lord directed his people to go to Egypt or why, having gone, they entered upon that period of intense suffering as slaves with which the book of Exodus opens. In Exodus 1 we begin to see that, in quiet, hidden ways, God is still on their side. In Exodus 2 we read of the start of his purpose to bring them out into liberty.

The savagery of the Egyptian royal house is seen in the edict to throw infant boys into the Nile (1:22), but out of that unfeeling house God brought a princess with a pitying heart!

Day 2. Read Exodus 2:23 – 3:10. Only God can help – and he will!

Governments come and go but there is no improvement in Israel's lot. But prayer proves to be the solution (2:23) – 'they cried ... God heard' – and he already had his agent at the ready: the discredited, fugitive Moses who had been an exile in Midian for the past 40 years. Humanly speaking he seemed on the scrap heap, but to God they were years of preparing him for the great act of leading Israel out of Egypt. The Lord who was preparing Moses knew all about his people's misery (3:7–9). Prayer is always answered, but in God's time and in his way.

Day 3. Read Exodus 13:17 – 14:22. The blessing of being under the cloud

To us, being 'under a cloud' means depression, disgrace. To Israel, the cloud was the greatest possible blessing and honour – God was with them, never leaving, always leading (13:21–22), moving to protect (14:19). This gave great assurance but not a trouble-free existence. They were taken what seemed the long way round (13:17,18), because the direct way would have proved too much for them to handle. They were led into a corner (14:2,9) so that they would experience the Lord's power to save and see the last of their enemies (14:13). God's ways, though often strange, are always purposeful and loving.

Day 4. Read Joshua 1:1–9. An unlikely leader, a guaranteed success

We are now forty years on. Through the sin of dis-obedience the journey to the promised land was prolonged by thirty-eight dreadful years. Moses is dead. Often the end of a long, dynamic period of leadership is the signal for everything to go into reverse. Not so! 'Moses is dead ...

Get ready to cross the Jordan' (verse 2). Joshua was the most unlikely leader, always needing reassurances (verses 5,9). But he was given a guaranteed way of success. The sin of disobedience had lost them the land before (Numbers 14:22,23), but undeviating attention and obedience to God's book would give them victory.

Day 5. Read Joshua 24:1–27. Responding to the Lord's goodness

Joshua's great campaigns of conquest are over. The land has yet to be settled by the tribes, but their enemies have been defeated and the land is theirs. Joshua reviews God's goodness (verses 5–12), and sums up in verse 13 – it has been all of God, his power, his determination. He has kept his promises. But now, what of their response? It should be one of reverence, sole devotion and service (verse 14). As always, our service is not a way into God's good books, but a response to his saving mercies already given. What a resounding example Joshua sets (verse 15)!

Day 6. Read Judges 2:9–23. A sad but encouraging pattern

Trace the pattern: sin (verse 11), divine displeasure (verse 12), punishment (verses 14,15), deliverance (verses 16–18), more sin and more divine anger (verse 19–20). This is the sad yet wonderful story of the book of Judges: a people ever-sinning, ever-defecting; a God ever-pitying, ever-saving. Have things changed at all? Have we? Has he?

Day 7. Read Judges 16:23–30. A failure – like all the rest

The story of Samson is compelling reading – such a buffoon of a man, never able to resist either a pretty face or a practical joke! A sad figure about whom it was said at the start 'he will begin to deliver' (13:5), and at the end that was all he did: beginnings without any conclusions. At the end of his life the great joker pulled his final practical joke, at the expense of his own life. What a warning of a wasted life! But all the judges were, in one way or another, the

same – partial, temporary deliverers bringing no final salvation. The book of Judges awaits the coming of the true
King and Saviour, the Lord Jesus Christ.

Week 3: Saul, David and Solomon

Day 1. Read 1 Samuel 1:1–3; 3:1–10. Another side to the story

The book of Judges, especially chapters 17 – 21, paints a
grim picture of people sinking into corruption. But there is
another side – a family who kept the flag of faith flying –
the godly, bluff Elkanah with his annual pilgrimages to
worship. To him and the attractive Hannah was born Samuel. How moving is the story of the way this young boy
came to know the Lord in a personal way! The Lord came
patiently calling and at last Samuel responded for himself.
He had been religious, occupied in religious things (3:1),
but 'Samuel did not yet know the Lord' (3:7), and the Lord
was not content with less than a personal response.

Day 2. Read 1 Samuel 8:1–6; 10:17–25. A new solution – a king!

The life of trusting God is often a strain. Doubt creeps in:
he helped me last time but will he do it again? That was
why they asked for a king. The Lord had previously saved
them, raising up judges in times of crisis, but would he
always do so? Wouldn't an institution like a monarchy be
better? Then there would always be someone to take a lead
against enemies. And the Lord graciously condescended
and gave them a lovely man named Saul. Note 10:25 – all
now depends on whether the new king obeys the 'rule of
success' (Joshua 1:7,8; see Week 2, Day 4).

Day 3. Read 1 Samuel 15:1–23. 'To obey is better'

In the hand of God, history, the story of human life on
earth, contains its elements of discipline and punishment
as well as those of divine generosity and bounty. Saul was
sent on a punitive mission against the savage Amalekites
(verses 1–3). However awesome their punishment sounds

28

to us, it was a solemn decree of absolute divine justice. To Saul, however, it was also a test of obedience. He failed . . . and lost his kingdom. Saul's is a heart-breaking story: an attractive man with immense gifts of inspiring love and loyalty, but he did not obey the word of the Lord.

Day 4. Read 1 Samuel 16:1–13. Chosen and equipped but . . .

This is how David came to be king, and forty chapters of the Bible now focus on him. One of the most extraordinary things about this unusual man is what immediately follows our passage: a catalogue of disasters! In quick succession he was courtier, soldier, outlaw and exile. Doesn't God move in strange ways? He chooses David to be king and then allows him to become 'public enemy number one'! Truly his ways are not our ways (Isaiah 55:8). David has a hard road to tread and difficult lessons of trust to learn.

Day 5. Read 1 Samuel 30:1–6; 2 Samuel 2:1–7. Touching bottom

Poor David. In all the miseries of exile there was one place to call home – Ziklag. But he returned to find it a heap of ruins, his family captured and his devoted followers ready to kill him. How do we react to such a blow? 'David found strength in the Lord his God' (30:6). Then he found it to be true (Psalm 113:7,8) that the distance from the ash heap to the throne is short (2:7) – a king at last! The Lord who brings down, brings up; not until we have been brought low can we be entrusted with the heights.

Day 6. Read 2 Samuel 7:1–22. David's everlasting house

How can we read this passage without reaching forward to Luke 1:30–33 where the story ends? How marvellous are God's ways! David, of course, did not know all this, but he was overwhelmed with gratitude for what he did know: he set out to build a house for the Lord only to find that the Lord planned to build a lasting royal house for him! In its way this is what the Old Testament is all about – the search and the wait for the perfect King. And now he has come, the Lord Jesus Christ.

Day 7. Read 1 Kings 3:1–15; 11:1–6. Another brilliant failure

The Old Testament never did find the perfect king, not even in Solomon. Truly the Lord gave him unique wisdom and, as with all God's gifts, along with it came those things that would test it. Would he develop the character to sustain his wisdom in the face of the testings of wealth, the applause of people ('honour', 3:13) and the tendency of old men to become old fools? No king ever had such a chance to be the perfect king, and none collapsed so signally. With the Old Testament examples before us we know that our salvation cannot be in man. We need someone greater than Solomon (Matthew 12:42).

Week 4: King after king. Kings of all sorts. Human failure

Day 1. Read 1 Kings 12:1–20. Goodbye David

What destroyed Rehoboam? In a word, arrogance. He couldn't be told! The story of Solomon shows that human character cannot stand life's testings. Rehoboam tells us that youthful assurance is not the answer either. Solomon the wise fell to folly; Rehoboam the confident fell to over-confidence. These kings teach us self-distrust; they are mirrors of the human heart. It is not 'There but for the grace of God go I', but simply 'There go I'. May the revelation of weakness drive us to seek God's grace!

Day 2. Read 2 Kings 9:1–28. It is not enough to be gifted

Following the disastrous Rehoboam, David's kingdom split into two: the ten tribes of 'Israel' or 'Ephraim' to the north, the two tribes of 'Judah' to the south. The northern kings raised themselves to the throne by their natural gifts: ambitious, able men aiming for the top. Jehu is typical: a brilliant commander (see how readily his peers offer him loyalty, verse 13), but what a ruthless brute of a man! No salvation for God's people here!

Day 3. Read 2 Kings 22:1–13; 23:24–26. It is not even enough to reform

Josiah is typical of the best of the south. Born in David's line, inheritor and custodian of the Lord's promises to David, he was well set for success by the discovery of the lost book. Now the kingdom could be governed by God's word. But what about the past? Before the good Josiah, his terrible father Manasseh has dropped a brick into the pool of history; Josiah rectified much of his father's error, but he could not hold back the swelling ripples in the pool (23:26). The people of God need a king who can deal with their past as well as their present and future. Only Jesus is such a king.

Day 4. Read 2 Kings 24:18 – 25:21. Name without reality

'Zedekiah' means 'The Lord is [my] righteousness', but the king was not that sort of man at all. He 'did evil in the eyes of the Lord' (24:19), and that, to the Lord, was the last straw. We cannot read the story of the destruction of old Jerusalem without a pang of sadness – all the glory of David and Solomon brought to the dust! But we must face the truth, and the Old Testament is there to teach it to us, that we must not deceive ourselves. God is not mocked; what people sow, they reap (Galatians 6:7). Not even precious Jerusalem, the city the Lord himself chose, is immune from this dread law.

Day 5. Read Ezra 1:1–11. A movement of the heart

Seventy years have passed since Jerusalem was destroyed. The Lord's people are exiles (but otherwise not greatly oppressed) in Babylon. They cannot have heard with equanimity, in the years prior to 539 BC, that a greater conqueror, Cyrus, was on his way. Surely this could only spell further bondage and prolonged exile! To think like this is to reckon without God. He is the Lord of all hearts (verses 1,5).

Day 6. Read Ezra 3:1–13. First things first

Try to feel the excitement of the returned community: back home and the great day of festal gathering to recommence worship! What was their first commitment? To obey the word of the Lord (verses 2,4,5): all must be done as it is written, required and appointed. What was their first act? To set up the altar (verse 2). The temple area was not yet cleared of rubble, the house itself not yet rebuilt, but first they set up the altar, the place where the atoning sacrifices were made; first and foremost is the need to be right with God through the blood sacrifices he has appointed.

Day 7. Read Nehemiah 1:1–11. Another 'first thing' first

The Persian Empire is now supreme in all lands. Nehemiah, in far off Susa, learns from eyewitnesses how desolate Jerusalem is, and the Lord stirs his heart to put things right. No small undertaking for a courtier to turn builder! So what did he do first? He made use of the often neglected, frequently despised, power of prayer and, according to the dates given in his book (1:1; 2:1), the Lord kept him at his prayers for three months before opening the door of opportunity to speak to the king. It is not a bad point at which to conclude our tour: a praying man, looking forward to the city of God.

2

The Voice of Religion

'Religion', says Chambers English Dictionary, 'is recognition of a higher, unseen, controlling power.' Yes, indeed, but there's more to it than that. Religion goes beyond merely 'recognizing' a higher power. It is also responding to that power in acts and ceremonies. If the god is thought of in savage terms, then religion will take savage forms. So what about the Old Testament?

God dwelling among his people

In Numbers 2 we are told how the camp of Israel was planned:

NORTH

WEST

EAST

Naphtali
Asher
Dan

Benjamin
Manasseh
Ephraim

Judah
Issachar
Zebulun

Reuben
Simeon
Gad

SOUTH

Actions speak louder than words! Could anything display more clearly that this God is one who chooses to live right at the heart of his people's life, and not only among them, but also actually sharing their lot? For these were camping days; the people of God were on the march to Canaan from their slavery in Egypt, and to this tent-dwelling people the Lord said, 'Make a tent for me and put it right at the centre of your camp.'

For the Lord's tent we often use the traditional name, 'the Tabernacle', but it was only a 'tent'! They were tent-dwellers and their God chose to be a tent-dweller with them, right at the heart of their life.

Later, in the days of Solomon, the tent was replaced by a house (1 Kings 6:1; NIV 'temple' should be 'house') but the message was the same. The people now had houses and, once again, their God made his will known that he too would have a house and live among them. The house of the Lord in the Old Testament was not really like what we call a 'church' (meaning church building) today, even though we do refer to our church as 'the house of God'. Today, as his people, we 'go to church' in order to be with him. In the Old Testament he came to his house in order to be among his people. He 'indwelt' them by having his own house among their houses.

Haggai's message

Now look at the message of the prophet Haggai. By his time the temple Solomon built was in ruins, and had been so for seventy years since the Babylonians demolished it in 586 BC, when the people went into exile in Babylon. But when Babylon fell in 539 BC to Cyrus the Persian, he allowed them to return (Ezra 1:1–3). After nineteen years back in their own land, however, this is what Haggai's perceptive prophetic eye saw (Haggai 1:6):

• The economy was in poor shape: 'You have planted much, but have harvested little.'
• The people were dissatisfied: 'You eat, but never have

enough. You drink but never have your fill. You put on clothes, but are not warm.'

● Inflation was rampant: 'You earn wages, only to put them in a purse with holes in it.'

What was the cause of this catalogue of such modern-sounding ills?: 'This house remains a ruin' (Haggai 1:4).

It was nearly twenty years since the exiles had been brought home from Babylon. In this time they had not done badly. They were living in panelled houses (Haggai 1:4), *i.e.* stone houses with an inner lining of timber – the ancient equivalent of cavity wall insulation! But the Lord's house was still unbuilt! It was still unrestored from the rubble of the Babylonian onslaught of getting on for a century earlier!

So, was Haggai just concerned with 'bricks and mortar'? Or was he simply a ritualist, offended because the full temple ceremonial was not possible while the temple was in ruins? It was neither of these things, but rather that, if people were not concerned to secure the living presence of the living God among them in the way that he had appointed, then they were opting for life without his presence (and blessing). They were choosing a go-it-alone life style, a do-it-yourself society. If they didn't want him they would have to do without what only he can supply.

What a message for Haggai's day – and our's! It does help us to see how seriously the Lord takes this matter of having a house among his people and living there. He comes, not as an ornament or as a passive spectator, but as the source of his people's well-being, prosperity and fulfil-ment. Indeed, Haggai says that once they began to build the house everything changed:

> Give careful thought to the day when the
> foundation of the Lord's temple was laid . . . From
> this day on I will bless you (Haggai 2:18,19).

The Lord God was once more dwelling among his people!

At home but not at home

Yet it is not all plain sailing to have God as one's neighbour! In the second half of the book of Exodus, the details of the 'Tabernacle' (the Lord's tent among his people's tents) are spelled out twice over, first as a list of what was needed for the tent (Exodus 25 – 31), and then as a description of how the work was done (Exodus 35 – 40). Tremendous emphasis is laid on the fact of the Lord's dwelling among them, the preparation that must be made for his coming, and the detailed care taken to have everything just as he wanted it (*cf.* Exodus 25:9).

The Lord promised to come into his tent and meet his people: 'There I will meet you ... I will dwell among the Israelites and be their God' (Exodus 29:42,45). This was the whole purpose of bringing them out of Egypt: '[I] brought them out of Egypt so that I might dwell among them' (Exodus 29:46).

Yet when all was finished and the Tabernacle pitched for the first time, and when the Lord in his glory had indeed come into his tent, we read: 'Moses could not enter the Tent of Meeting because the cloud had settled upon it, and the glory of the Lord filled the tabernacle' (Exodus 40:35).

Not even Moses, then what price the rest of us! The Lord was indeed at home among his people but not 'at home' to callers!

The Lord's cloud

In Exodus 3 Moses came face to face with the Lord for the first time. It is the famous incident of 'the burning bush' as we call it, but in reality the bush did not burn at all!

> ... the angel of the Lord appeared to him in [or
> 'as'] flames [better 'a flame'] of fire from within a
> bush. Moses saw that though the bush was on fire
> it did not burn up (Exodus 3:2).

Here was an unusual thing – a flame that did not need fuel to feed it, a self-perpetuating flame! A *living* flame! And as soon as Moses approached, the divine voice alerted him to two things: first, that the flame symbolized the divine presence; secondly, that in particular the flame stood for the holiness of God (Exodus 3:2–5).

The story of the flame of fire continues at Mount Sinai: 'Mount Sinai was covered with smoke, because the Lord descended on it in fire' (Exodus 19:18). Commentators have been known to 'explain' what happened at Sinai as volcanic action, but the Exodus account contradicts this, for here was not a fire that belched upwards but a fire that came down: 'The Lord descended to the top of Mount Sinai' (Exodus 19:20).

The message is the same as at the 'burning bush': the holy God has come among his people. Hence the command: 'Put limits around the mountain and set it apart as holy' (Exodus 19:23).

To be sure, God was down among them but, once more, his holiness kept them at a distance.

Always the 'Sinai people'

As soon as the Tabernacle was prepared, the stay at Sinai was over, but though they left the actual mountain behind, they carried the reality of Sinai with them: the holy God now lived among his people. The cloud on the Tabernacle held at its heart the very fire of God (Exodus 40:35,38). The Tabernacle stood and was carried at the centre of the people (Numbers 2:17; 10:21).

God was with them and travelled with them, but he is the Holy One and they must keep their distance. What does this 'holiness' mean?

If we draw a diagram of the Tabernacle from the details given in Exodus 25 – 31 it looks like this:

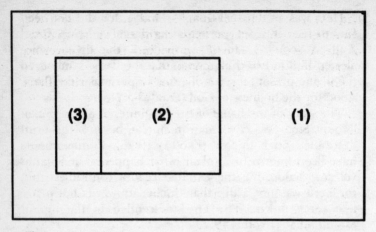

There was (1) the outer Courtyard; (2) the 'holy place', the first compartment of the tent itself; and (3) the 'holy of holies', 'the Most Holy Place' (Exodus 26:31–33). In this 'Most Holy Place' Moses was told to put, as its sole piece of furniture, 'the Ark of the Lord' containing the stone tablets of the Ten Commandments (Exodus 25:10–22). That was all. In pagan religions those who penetrated into the inner-most sanctuary came face to face with some idol, but in the Tabernacle they came face to face with the moral law.

This was the reason no-one could enter: no-one was worthy! The holiness of the God of Israel is the moral holiness which the Commandments express as his standard for our lives (Leviticus 19:2). Until something is done to satisfy the demands of that law and to deal with the way we have broken it, the door into God's presence must remain shut in our faces.

The holy God: provider of sacrifice

So 'none could enter', but this is not the whole truth. The letter to the Hebrews summarizes the Old Testament exactly when it says: 'But only the high priest entered the inner room, and that only once a year, and never without blood' (Hebrews 9:7).

The 'Ark', the box containing the Ten Commandments,

had a very special lid (Exodus 25:17–22). It was called 'the atonement cover' and had to match the exact measurement of the Ark itself (verse 17), providing an exact covering over the holy law the Ark contained.

The name 'atonement cover' both describes what it did and also explains what it was for. The Hebrew verb 'to cover' means just that, as when Noah 'covered' his ark (a different word for 'ark') with pitch (Genesis 6:14). But in Old Testament religion the word developed a new, additional meaning. Sometimes when we hand over money to pay a bill, we say, 'You'll find that that covers it': the payment 'covers' the debt, not by hiding it out of sight (like pitch on the woodwork of the ark) but by cancelling it out altogether.

This is how God provides 'atonement' for our sin: a price is paid that 'covers' the debt, not sweeping it under the carpet, but cancelling it out by a full and equivalent payment.

Passover: the blood of the lamb

We can think about this important truth in two ways: first through an event which illustrates it, and secondly through a verse in which it is taught.

The event is the Passover. In Exodus 12 the situation is that the Lord plans to enter Egypt in judgment (verse 12), and the story answers the question how we can be safe at such a time. Three words tell it all: the first is the word 'satisfaction'. The Israelites were instructed that, in preparation for this night of divine judgment, they were to smear the blood of a sacrificed lamb around their doors (verse 7), relying on the Lord's promise that, 'The blood will be a sign for you on the houses where you are; and when I see the blood, I will pass over you' (verse 13). Not 'when I see you', as if safety from divine judgment was an act of favouritism. No, there is something about the blood that turns the Lord from judgment to peace, and satisfies him regarding the people in the blood-marked houses.

The second word is a counterpart of the first: 'safety'.

Since God is satisfied, the people are safe (verse 23) for, he promises, while the people remain where the blood was shed there is no way the Destroyer can come in to hurt them.

But these two words demand an explanation: what is it about this blood that satisfies God and keeps his people safe? Verses 3 and 4 begin to point to the answer. The lamb chosen had to match exactly both the number of the people in each house and also their needs ('what each person will eat'). There is, in this way, an exact equivalence between the animal that died and the people who take shelter under its blood.

But according to verse 30, 'There was loud wailing in Egypt, for there was not a house without someone dead.' Divine judgment on those who had refused to obey God's word took the token but dreadful form of the death in each Egyptian house of the firstborn son. In the houses of Israel the dead body was that of the carefully selected lamb. Our third word is, therefore, 'substitution'. The death of a substitute 'covered' Israel in the day of judgment for, says Exodus 4:22, 'Israel is my firstborn son'.

The verse in which this lovely truth is taught is Leviticus 17:11. Speaking of the animal designated for sacrifice it says:

> The life of a creature is in the blood, and I have
> given it to you to make atonement ['to pay the
> covering price'] for yourselves on the altar; [for] it
> is the blood that makes atonement ['pays the
> covering price'] for ['as the equivalent to'] one's
> life.

Look carefully at this verse. It teaches: that one life is laid down as the equivalent of another; that this is the gift of God; that the heart of the matter is the payment of the covering price. When the covering price is paid the debt is discharged and gone for ever.

The Day of Atonement

Once every year the high priest made atonement for the whole community (Leviticus 16). Two animals and two ceremonies were involved. One was hidden away within the Tabernacle; the other was public, for all to see.

Since the real problem of our sin is the broken law of God and offence given to him as the Holy One, our first need is to bring the shed blood before him. So, for the one and only time in the year, the High Priest, carrying the blood of the sin-offering (16:15) went beyond the separating curtain into the Most Holy place and the 'atonement-cover', the exact covering of the law that had been broken, received the blood of a life laid down for the sins of the people.

All this was hidden away, however, and the Lord wanted his people to see, before their very eyes, the meaning and value of what had happened out of sight in his presence behind the curtain. So he ordered a second ceremony in which the High Priest laid his hands on the head of another beast and confessed over it all the people's sins (16:20–22). In this way he put their sins on the head of another. The animal became a sin-bearer; the sins of the guilty passed to the account of the innocent. And as the people watched, the sin-bearing beast carried all their sins right away, never to be seen again.

At the Day of Atonement this was a communal exercise, but exactly the same thing happened individually and personally in every one of the sacrifices (e.g. Leviticus 1:4; 3:2; 4:4,24,29). The Lord's provision was wonderful, simple and merciful. The sinner identified the animal with his guilt and need before God; one died in the place of another; and atonement was made. This is the beating heart of Old Testament religion.

**A Scenic Route Through
Old Testament Religion**

———————

**Meet the Old Testament church in its public religious
observances and meet its members as they walked with
God**

Four weeks of short daily Bible readings with brief notes

Week 1: The holy God living among his people

Day 1. Read Exodus 29:42–46. A lovely divine purpose

Up to this point the book of Exodus has made three things plain: (a) With patience and power the Lord brought his people out of Egyptian slavery; (b) there was little that was attractive about them: they resisted his word, grumbled at his ways, even regretted he had brought them out at all; (c) the tent (the Tabernacle) in which God wished to dwell is described by God in great detail (Exodus 25 – 31). This tent (says today's passage) was the very reason he brought them out and bore with them, *so that he might dwell among them!* They were a people in tents; so he would be a camping God with his tent among theirs. He is a God near at hand, sharing our lot, bearing with our oddities, available for our needs (Ephesians 2:19–22).

Day 2. Read 2 Samuel 7:1–3, 12, 13. Still the same: the Lord among his people

400 years have passed but God remains the same. David is now on the throne and his instincts tell him, correctly, that the God who lived in a mobile home, when his people were travelling people, would now wish to have his house among their houses. No wonder Nathan promptly agreed: the Lord the Bible reveals is always the indwelling Lord, at hand, with and among us. But he is still the Lord: he does things his way and the time is not yet right (with verse 9

42

read Deuteronomy 12:10,11), the man is not right (with verse 5 read 1 Chronicles 22:8 – the man of war cannot build the house of peace). But by all this we see that it is not man's will to provide a house and (so to speak) 'organize' the Lord's presence with us; it is his will that he should come to live where we live.

Day 3. Read 1 Kings 8:12–13, 17–21, 27–29. Very wonderful. Very true

Note the central thought in each short passage: Verses 12–13, what is the house for? The God whom we could never discover or find for ourselves (hidden in thick darkness) comes to live among his people. Verses 17–21, it is *his* purpose to do so; that is why he kept his promise to give David a son and heir. His 'name' (verse 20) is shorthand for 'all that the Lord has revealed about himself', *i.e.* God in the fulness of his revealed character comes to dwell in the house! Verses 27–29, yes, he really does! The heavens are too small to contain his greatness, yet he has undertaken that his 'name' will dwell in the house. He will fully and truly live 'down among' his people.

Day 4. Read Exodus 40:34–38. Strange – but it stands to reason!

In the book of Exodus all the details of the Lord's tent are given twice over. First, everything is described (chapters 25 – 31) and then everything is done as described (chapters 35 – 40). Finally the day came when everything was exactly right, just as the Lord wished it, and true to his word, he came visibly in the cloud which signified 'God is here', to take up residence among his people. But not even Moses could enter where the Lord was (verse 35). The Lord was at home but not 'at home' to callers. For when he comes, he comes as he is, in all the fulness of his holy nature, and how could we possibly enter and come before the Holy One? We can't. It stands to reason.

Day 5. Read Exodus 3:1–5. Moses' experience: shut out . . . let in

What a vivid scene! The flame of fire in the bush. A unique flame that needed no fuel to feed on: the bush was only the dwelling place of a flame that was self-sufficient, full of life all its own. The voice from the bush explained that this represented the threatening holiness of God which Moses dare not approach. As we saw yesterday, the Lord's holiness is not a passive beauty, but an active force that threatens and excludes all that offends it. But here is something wonderful: Moses is told a simple thing to do whereby he will be safe and accepted. Take off his shoes! As we shall learn, this too is true of the God of the Bible: it is like him to make a simple provision whereby we can enter and enjoy the fellowship of the Holy One (see John 14:6).

Day 6. Read Isaiah 6:1–5. Isaiah's experience: a threatening holiness

Uzziah had reigned fifty-two years. As the old king's life slipped away, was Isaiah comforted by the thought that though kings have to go, the King (verse 1, 'the Lord', 'The Sovereign') remains? If so, the comfort soon passed, for the seraphim were proclaiming the holiness of God. Hebrew repeats a word in order to emphasize it. This is the only case where an attribute is stated three times: the holiness of the Lord is super-superlative! It is a sobering thought that a sin we might have dismissed as pretty negligible, a sin of speech, blots out the vision of God and prompts Isaiah's conviction that he is doomed.

Day 7. Read Isaiah 6:6–8. Isaiah's experience: the way home to God

When the cloud blotted out everything else, the altar and its flaming embers remained in view. The coal which was pressed to the place where Isaiah knew himself to be a sinner represented all that the altar stood for – a sacrifice to God making atonement, covering our sin, bringing forgiveness and reconciliation. The words of the seraph explain this: iniquity and sin are taken away, the price has been paid and Isaiah, who first saw the Lord only afar off (verse 1), and then was excluded from his presence altogether (verses 4,5), is now, because forgiven, brought into his close fellowship, into a speaking relationship with the holy God.

Week 2: 'Not without blood': the sacrifices and their meaning

Day 1. Read Exodus 12:1–6. The carefully selected lamb

The people were slaves in Egypt, doomed to death. The Lord's command to 'take a lamb' could well have seemed totally irrelevant, but it was in fact the key to their redemption and freedom. The Lord had promised not only to bring them out *from* Egypt but to bring them *to* himself (Exodus 6:6,7), for there is no true freedom unless people are at peace with God. As a first step he required them to select a lamb very carefully so that it exactly represented the number and the needs of the people of God (verse 4). Its 'perfection' made it acceptable to God (verse 5). This was the lamb that was destined to die (verse 6).

Day 2. Read Exodus 12:7–13. Peace with God

Every verse in this passage is important but most of all verse 13. The blood of the lamb (symbolizing its death) has been sprinkled (verse 7). The people are inside the blood-marked houses and are at the ready, dressed for the journey (verse 11). The Lord enters Egypt as judge and executioner (verse 12) but, seeing the blood, has no case to pursue or judgment to execute against those sheltering there (verse 13). Is it daring to say that the blood 'changes' God? The fact is that when he sees the blood, wrath is gone and he 'passes over' in peace. This is what John meant when he pointed to Jesus as 'the Lamb of God' (John 1:29,36), and what Paul meant when he said we have peace with God through 'the blood of his cross' (Colossians 1:20).

Day 3. Read Exodus 12:21–24. The sheltered people

These verses emphasize what we already know from verse 13. Those who have entered where the blood of the lamb was shed are safe. Note how verses 22 and 23 keep coming back to 'the blood' – that is the vital matter. The lamb has died, and, as we saw on Day 1, the lamb was equivalent to the number and needs of the people on the one hand and, in its perfection, acceptable to God on the other. The holy Judge is satisfied when the lamb, equivalent to his people, has died. What the Passover depicts in this way is the central truth of the Bible (not just the Old Testament) about atonement and peace with God. In the wise and merciful plan of God, the perfect dies in the place of the needy so that we may enjoy peace with a satisfied God.

Day 4. Read Leviticus 16:15–17. Making atonement: the unseen reality

In the tent (Tabernacle) in which the Lord lived among his people, the inner shrine was only entered once a year. On the Day of Atonement the High Priest brought in there the blood of the sin offering and sprinkled it before God, making atonement 'for himself, his household and the whole community of Israel' (verse 17). In this way proof was brought to God that the beast designated as a sin offering had died, and this death was accepted as paying for and thus covering all the sins of the people throughout the preceding year. 'Atonement' literally means 'covering', not simply in the sense of hiding away, but in the sense that payment 'covers' a debt – paying and cancelling.

Day 5. Read Leviticus 16:20–22. The sin-bearer, the visible demonstration

The Lord wanted his people to know what it was that had happened in the secrecy of the inner shrine, so a second and public ceremony was appointed. When Aaron laid his hands on the chosen beast and confessed Israel's sins, we read that he put them on the head of the goat (verse 21), and the goat bore all their iniquities away – a vivid picture of the innocent taking the place of the guilty, accepting as his own their offences, and bearing them away never to be seen again. This is what all the atoning sacrifices meant: they were *substitutionary* (one taking the place of another) and *sin-bearing* (one accepting and removing the sin of another). In every case the payment was a life laid down. The Lord Jesus himself taught us to understand his death in exactly this way (Mark 10:45). Consequently this is how the New Testament understands the cross (*e.g.* 1 Timothy 2:5, 6; 1 Peter 2:24; 3:18).

Day 6. Read Leviticus 1:3–9. The offering that holds nothing back

Besides the sin offering, one of the main offerings appointed by God was the burnt offering. When Abraham was called to offer Isaac, it was as a burnt offering (Genesis 22:2). His readiness to do so proved that he had 'not withheld' anything God required (Genesis 22:12). Like all the offerings this involved (a) laying hands on the animal, *i.e.* appointing the animal as a substitute (see Day 5); (b) making atonement by presenting the blood (verse 5); and (c) offering the entire beast as a sacrifice to God (verse 9). This means that when we belong to God by atonement, he looks to us to hold nothing back in our devoted obedience to him.

Day 7. Read Leviticus 3:12–16; 7:11–15. A shared joy

The third of the main offerings was the 'Peace Offering' or 'Fellowship Offering'. It was made on occasions of joy or thanksgiving or as an act of special devotion to the Lord. Part of it was burnt (3:16) and this is called 'food' – not as if they were feeding God, but to symbolize the fact that he came himself to share in his people's joy. Part was given to the priest (7:14), and the remainder was enjoyed by the worshipper that day – a command which necessitated inviting others to the party (Deuteronomy 16:11), for who alone could eat the rest of a whole beast? This sacrifice involved personal, family and communal joy, resting on and arising out of atonement, peace with God.

Week 3: Ritual and response; religion and holiness

Day 1. Read Malachi 1:6–10. Only the best for the Lord

Malachi's topic is plain enough: it is so easy to come to regard religious observance as an end in itself, especially with a religion like that of the Old Testament where so many rituals were obligatory. Malachi's people had fallen into the snare of thinking that somehow these rituals, simply as performances, were pleasing to the Lord. But it is never so! Ceremonies impose demands on the worshipper, for religious observance begins in the heart. Since actions speak louder than words, it was the way they behaved which showed that they despised his name and said his table was contemptible. But the Lord would rather not have the ritual than have it without the heart's devotion and commitment of his people.

Day 2. Read Jeremiah 7:4–11. No benefit without commitment

The temple and its services were ordained by God (verse 4), but Jeremiah found people thinking that just because the temple stood there, and its services were performed, they were somehow safe from every threat; they were keeping in God's good books! But there is no true religion without mending our ways (verse 5). They were in fact treating the Lord's house as robbers treat their 'den' (verse 11), a place to go to for safety and then come out from it every bit as much robbers and villains as when they went in! When we think of the main offerings noted in last week's readings, what is the point of the sin offering without repentance and hatred of sin? Or of the burnt offering without 'holding nothing back' from God?

Day 3. Read Amos 5:21–25. Keeping the balance right

It must have sounded simply dreadful to hear Amos say that the Lord hated the religious services which he had himself ordained: feasts, gatherings, offerings, worship –

all detestable! So they are if they are divorced from living justly and righteously (verse 24). The question in verse 25 implies 'Was it *sacrifices* you brought me? Was that *all*?' Yes indeed, they had brought sacrifices, but they had also brought obedience to the Lord's law given at Sinai. Religion went hand in hand with obedience to God's word. The truths of these three days' readings are for us too. The religion of the Bible is all of a piece. We have our God-ordained services and worship. Sadly we too can become slipshod and second rate (Day 1); lacking moral commitment (Day 2); and forgetful of the balance between the means of grace and the responsive life of obedience (Day 3).

Day 4. Read Exodus 24:4–8. A picture of the true

The picture is self-explanatory (verse 4): the Lord has kept his promise of Exodus 6:6,7. He has gathered his people into his presence. Moses sprinkled the blood on the altar (verse 6), because it is the sprinkled blood that makes peace with God. Only around a bloodstained altar are the Lord's people in fellowship with him. But watch what happened next: (a) those who are at peace with God are called to hear his word and obey it (verse 7); (b) because our obedience at best is a patchy affair with many false starts, many slips and much left undone, we need the cleansing blood as our constant covering (verse 8). See 1 John 1:7 – as we 'walk' (our daily life of obedience) in his way, the blood of Jesus goes on cleansing us.

Day 5. Read Psalm 32:1–7. The way of repentance

The psalm does not specifically link itself with the time when David committed adultery with Bathsheba and secured the death of her husband, but verse 5 is the perfect poetic counterpart of 2 Samuel 12:13. God's law provided no atoning sacrifice for adultery and murder, only the death penalty. But David found that by truly repenting, even these sins could be forgiven! This is the effectiveness of simple penitence. By this means we enter into forgiveness (verse 1), a clear account before God (verse 2), and the misery of the sinner (verse 3) is replaced by the song of one who has been delivered (verse 7).

Day 6. Read Isaiah 1:11–20. The way of obedience

Once more a prophet exposes the hollowness before God of a 'prayer wheel' religion – keeping the ritual in motion whilst neglecting personal holiness. In their gatherings the Lord saw an unholy mixture, (verse 13, literally 'wickedness along with religious dutifulness'); when they prayed he could not hear the words they said because he was looking at their hands, stained with many an uncleansed, unrepented sin (verse 15). But the remedy was available: in verse 16, the first verb 'wash' implies 'make use of the religious ceremonies of purification'; the second verb 'make . . . clean' means 'bring about a moral reformation' – the life of obedience to God's word (verse 19). Obeying him is the proper outcome of his offer of cleansing (verse 18).

Day 7. Read Amos 7:7–9. The enduring foundation

The wall Amos saw is the wall of our life as we have been, and are, building it. 'Built true to plumb' (NIV) is literally 'Built with a plumbline', i.e. the plumbline was available to the builder all day long. But it is now to be tested by the Lord's plumbline. From the start of building the people had (as we have) both God's law to obey and God's grace to cleanse (see Day 4). The true, God-intended life of the Lord's people (then and now) stands straight and firm when it rests always on his forgiving grace and is committed to obey his holy law.

Week 4: Walking with God

Day 1. Read Micah 6:6–8. The acceptable life

Micah asks three questions: (a) What brings us into God's presence? (verse 6); (b) what brings us into God's favour? ('Will the Lord be pleased?' verse 7); (c) what brings us into God's peace? (how do I deal with my sin? verse 7). The answer is: not 'going over the top' in the use of ritual (verses 6,7); not going beyond what the Lord asks (verse 7), but just 'what is good' (verse 8). This involves the required sacrifices in the context of (a) living a just life ('act justly'); (b) having a true devotion ('love mercy', *i.e.* 'maintain steadfast love' to God and man); (c) keeping humble fellowship with God. In this threefold prescription we see how very personal was the religious life of the Old Testament, and of the Bible.

Day 2. Read Deuteronomy 16:16,17. The routine of true religion

Elkanah went yearly to Shiloh (1 Samuel 1:3); Joseph and Mary went yearly to Jerusalem (Luke 2:41). This annual pilgrimage was costly in time, money and effort. But the Lord's actual requirement was three times a year: 'Unleavened bread', the popular name for Passover, when they came to remember their redemption; 'weeks', at the start of the harvest season, later called Pentecost, a feast of joy because bondage in Egypt was past (verses 11,12); 'Tabernacles', when the full harvest was home, remembering God's provision and care in the wilderness days. All three feasts were a special entrance into the Lord's presence (verse 16), and a chance to express devotion in proportionate giving (verse 17). No lukewarm religion this!

Day 3. Read Daniel 6:1–10; Psalm 55:16,17. Keeping in touch

Daniel's life was that of a top civil servant in a huge empire, but he made time for his personal prayer. He was threatened by jealousy, but did not forsake the discipline and joy of three daily periods of quiet with God. David's life was such that, given a chance, he would have grown wings and flown away (Psalm 55:6,7). But though wings were impossible, flight was not, and he flew to God three times a day – as the day ended, as it began, and in the heart of its midday pressures. How very slack we allow ourselves to be!

Day 4. Read 1 Samuel 1:4–17. The wonder of prayer and the rest it brings

Elkanah did his good-humoured best but what Hannah

needed was not 'Am I not better to you than ten sons?' (verse 8), but 'Dear Hannah, you are better to me than ten sons.' And in addition to being childless, Hannah had to put up with Peninnah and her ceaseless teasing. So she took it to the Lord in prayer and when she returned from the place of prayer every thing except one was still the same: she was still childless, Peninnah was still teasing, Elkanah was still his uncomprehending self, but her heart was no longer sad (verse 18). Prayer does change things.

Day 5. Read Jeremiah 12:1–5. Telling God to his face!
There is a blunt straightness about much Old Testament praying. The people knew the Lord well enough to vent their frustrations on him, rather than retiring hurt and chewing the fat to themselves. Jeremiah believed rightly that God is absolutely righteous (verse 1), but there was so much in the world that seemed downright unjust and unfair (verses 1,2), for look how life treated Jeremiah who served God with all his might (verse 3)! Hannah (see yesterday) took her sorrows to the Lord; Jeremiah took his problems with life to the Lord. Verse 5 is the Lord's reply: today's experiences are tomorrow's training ground. A good lesson to learn. And so is the lesson that we can explode to the Lord in our prayers.

Day 6. Read Numbers 6:1–8. Times of special commitment
A person became a Nazirite in order, for a fixed time, to show special devotion to the Lord (verse 1). Alcohol (verses 3,4) represented life's joys and the Nazirite would now seek all his joys in the Lord. Hair (verse 5) represented the output of bodily strength and all his vigour would now be for the Lord. Separation (verse 6) acknowledged the paramount claim of the Lord on time and relationships, even a family bereavement (verse 7). A Nazirite wanted to be holy, wholly for the Lord.

It is easy to say, but should we not be like that in principle all the time? Of course, yes! But the Old Testament is so practical. Life offers many attractive joys within the will of God, many calls on time and strength of which he would approve, many dear personal bonds of love which he gladly allows us. It is good to set aside a fixed time solely for him.

Day 7. Read Nehemiah 8:1–8. The people of the book

This is one of the last pictures we have of the Lord's people in the Old Testament. They are gathered round the word of God, unanimous and eager to hear the Bible (verse 1), recognizing an obligation that all who can understand will give their absorbed attention (verses 2,3), reverencing the word (verse 5), and listening to those who can make its meaning clear (verses 6–8). They know that this book was the product of human authorship (verse 1), nevertheless, it was the Lord's word: designed by him as 'law', his own 'teaching' for his people (verse 8). Such is the whole Bible to us.

3

The Voice of Worship

A window

The Psalms are our window into the Old Testament. We look through them and we actually see what it was like to be a believer in those old covenant times. What surprise and delight awaits us! Indeed the men and women of the Old Testament often put us to shame by the reality, the personal quality, the joy, exuberance and knowledge of God that is so clear in their worship and song.

Knowing God
Look how well they knew God. Here are some verses from Psalm 18. Read them slowly. Think about each word:

> I love you, O Lord, my strength.
> The Lord is my rock, my fortress and my
>   deliverer;
>   my God is my rock, in whom I take refuge.
> He is my shield and the horn of my salvation, my
>   stronghold.
> I call to the Lord, who is worthy of praise . . .
>   (18:1–3).

Corresponding to this deep knowledge of who and what God is, there is a matching spirit of devotion:

> I have chosen the way of truth;
>   I have set my heart on your laws.
> I run in the path of your commands . . .

Oh, how I love your law!
  I meditate on it all day long.
How sweet are your words to my taste,
  sweeter than honey to my mouth!
                    (119:30,32,97,103).

Or again, God was at the centre of their approach to life,
even in its severest testings. Psalm 74 is typical in two ways:
first, it faces up to the real awfulness of life. It does not
pretend that things are other or better than they are. But
then, in the teeth of that awfulness, it asserts what is true
about God:

Turn your steps towards these everlasting ruins,
  all this destruction the enemy has brought on
      the sanctuary . . .
But you, O God, are my king from of old;
  you bring salvation upon the earth (74:3,12).

School atlases used to go out of their way to make sure that
we knew the comparative size of each country. If England
and Australia can both fill the same-sized page, how were
children to know that the one was so immensely bigger
than the other? Well, in the corner of the Australia page
there would be a tiny, postage-stamp-sized England, with
the words, 'England on the same scale.'

The Psalms do the same thing but in reverse: alongside
the problems of life they set a huge reality, 'God on the
same scale'! This is what Psalm 74 is doing. Though its
problem looks like an 'everlasting ruin' that not all the time
in the world could mend, the great King is still on his
throne!

This approach to things is constant in the Psalms. Amid
an endless variety of earthly crises and challenges to faith –
national, personal, social and domestic, with problems of
inequality, suffering, injustice, depression and disappointment – each map of trouble is accompanied by another
which reduces it to its proper proportions: the greatness of
the Lord in position, power and salvation.

Prayer, forgiveness, hope and joy

Along with this grasp of the greatness of God goes a vigorous confidence in prayer:

> Hear my prayer, O Lord;
>> listen to my cry for mercy.
> In the day of my trouble I will call to you,
>> for you will answer me (86:6,7).

And there is so much more, but we must be content for the moment with three further aspects of the Psalms. First, the psalmists knew what it meant to be right with God. What about this regarding the forgiveness of sins?

> If you, O Lord, kept a record of sins,
>> O Lord, who could stand?
> But with you there is forgiveness . . .
>> with the Lord is unfailing love
>> and with him is full redemption (130:3–4,7).

But more, the Psalms were not afraid to say 'afterwards', pointing to the life to come:

> Yet I am always with you;
>> you hold me by my right hand.
> You guide me with your counsel,
>> and afterwards you will take me into glory . . .
> My flesh and my heart may fail,
>> but God is the strength of my heart
>> and my portion for ever (73:23,24,26).

And finally, what exuberance they enjoyed in worship!

> Clap your hands, all you nations;
>> shout to God with cries of joy.
> God has ascended amid shouts of joy,
>> the Lord amid the sounding of trumpets
>>> (47:1,5).

Praise him with tambourine and dancing,
    praise him with the strings and flute,
praise him with the clash of cymbals,
    praise him with resounding cymbals.
Let everything that has breath praise the Lord
                                        (150:4–6).

The content and origin of the Psalms

So often we look into the Old Testament through the
window of the Pharisees as we meet them in the New
Testament: joyless people, carping, critical, laden with the
dust of man-made tradition, their lives cramped and dis-
torted by human regulations (Matthew 15:3,6–9)! We need
to remember that the Lord Jesus spoke of the Pharisees as
'a plant his heavenly Father did not plant' (Matthew 15:13).
This means that far from being typical Old Testament
people, the Pharisees were, in relation to the Old Testament, what we would call 'heretics' and not 'Exhibit A' of
the Old Testament church at all!

No, it is in the Psalms that we see at first hand the real
Old Testament religion and worship with all its joyousness,
its delight and spiritual confidence, its true knowledge of
God and its simplicity of trust in him for time and eternity.

The passages already quoted show the way in which the
Psalms arose from actual experiences of life in both joy and
sorrow. One person's experiences, David's, loom very
large, but he was by no means the only one. Here are some
examples:

- *Experience of life:* joys (92,113); sorrows (42,88).
- *David's experiences:* personal (3,18,34); royal (101,110).
- *Religious experience:* processions (24,118); 'pilgrim praise'
  (120–134).

All this abundance of poetry and song is spread over
nearly a thousand years. Psalm 90 is attributed to Moses,
and very likely the title covers Psalm 91 also. At the other
end of the period stands Psalm 137 which looks back,

possibly from a fairly close vantage-point, to the experience of exile in Babylon.

In so far as it is possible to date the bulk of Psalms within
the history of Israel, it might look something like this:

1000 BC	586 BC	520 BC
David/Solomon ...... Reforming kings First Temple .... Temple recovery .... PILGRIM FEASTS	Exile	Return Second Temple
The Psalms of David Pilgrim Psalms (120–134, etc.) Kingship praise (93–100) Praise collections (113–118,146–150) Choir repertoires (42–49,72–83) The choirmaster collection (51–62, etc.)		THE BOOK OF PSALMS

This diagram oversimplifies very complicated questions
and there is so much we simply do not know. How were
individual psalms preserved? How were they edited into
groups and small collections, what we would call 'hymn
books'? Who was 'the choirmaster' (NIV 'director of
music') who is mentioned 55 times (*e.g.* Psalms 4,5,6) and
what did he do? Why are the psalms of David scattered as
they are? And why do the small 'hymnbooks' (*e.g.* 93–100;
120–134) appear where they do in the final Psalter?

On the other hand, in spite of all this ignorance, there is
no reason to doubt that the vast majority of the psalms
were written before the exile, or that the ascription (literally) 'To David' was intended to signify David's
authorship.

The first (Solomon's) temple
The period of the monarchy saw great 'reformations' of
religion under Asa (1 Kings 15:11–15); Jehoshaphat (1
Kings 22:41–47; 2 Chronicles 17:7–9; 19:4–11); Joash (2

Kings 11 – 12; 2 Chronicles 24); Hezekiah (2 Kings 18:1–4; 2 Chronicles 29 – 31); Josiah (2 Kings 22 – 23; 2 Chronicles 34 – 35). These refocused national life on the temple and it is sensible to think that they would have stimulated the collection of inherited worship songs for use in the reformed temple. Certainly the headings and the text of the Psalms suggest how they were used in worship. Psalm 45 (and many others) indicate the tune to be used; the word 'song' in the heading to Psalm 48 and elsewhere indicates musical accompaniment; the little word 'Selah' which is sprinkled throughout the Psalms (*e.g.* 46:3,7,11), has so far defied explanation both as a word and as to its use, but it was probably some sort of 'divider', maybe indicating a pause for meditation when the psalm was sung in worship.

The second (post-exilic) temple

By the time the second temple was built (Ezra 3; 6:13–22; Haggai 1 – 2) in 520–516 BC, there was a rich harvest of songs waiting to be gathered into a larger hymnbook, and we can attribute the production of the Psalter as we know it to the religious leaders at that time.

Worship

What is this worship of which the Psalms are the vocal expression? An easy way to get a taste (but no more than a taste) of worship in the Old Testament is through the key words which show us worship in action. From these we learn something very important indeed. Old Testament religion was often outwardly complicated, involving all the rituals of the book of Leviticus. Also it was often very exuberant and noisy. But at its centre there was a still, even solemn, heart of devotion, a wondering awareness of God and the realization that before such an awesome God only the lowest place befits his worshippers.

Psalm 95:6 gathers three such verbs together (reduced to two in NIV): 'Come, let us *bow* and *stoop down*; let us *kneel* before the Lord our Maker'. It is not important to try to make distinctions between the three verbs – their meanings are accurately reflected in this translation – but rather to

THE VOICE OF WORSHIP

feel their cumulative force as worshippers bring themselves down ('bow') and down lower ('stoop') and then lower still ('kneel').

Such was the reaction of Elijah before the awesomeness of 'the God who answered by fire' when he (literally) 'crouched on the ground' in acknowledgment, and in submissive waiting for God (1 Kings 18:24, 38,42).

In Psalm 95, however, it was not, as for Elijah, fire from heaven which prompted this self-humbling worship, but the works of God in salvation and providential care. He is our 'Maker' (verse 6) in the sense that by his choice, out of all who live on earth, he 'made' us his people. Having chosen to do so, he has never ceased to tend us as our Shepherd-God (verse 7), leading us from pasture to pasture, keeping us as (literally) 'the sheep of his hand'. In this way worship is a response to revealed truth: the truth of God our Saviour.

Responding: the Lord's name
Psalms 104:35 – 105:3 offer us a whole cluster of verbs of vocal response: *Bless* (NIV 'praise') the Lord, O my soul'; *praise* the Lord; *give thanks* to the Lord; *call* on his name; *sing* to him; *make music* (NIV 'sing praise') to him; *meditate* on all his wonders; *respond in praise* to his holy name.

Notice that twice in these verses the 'name' of the Lord is praised. His 'name' is shorthand for all that he has revealed himself to be. In other words, worship arises out of what the Lord has said about himself. It is not governed by human tradition (*cf.* Mark 7:5–7), nor by what we may from time to time 'find helpful' (*cf.* Amos 4:4,5), but only by the revelation of his name and what he has done (his 'wonders' performed in the salvation of his people).

Blessing the Lord
Meditating on these truths leads us to praise God for himself and for his works, and to give thanks for the heavenly benefits he has given us. The lovely expression 'to bless the Lord' has sadly disappeared from the NIV and yet it seems to have a very special meaning. When the Lord

61

'blesses' us (the same word is used) he reviews what we are
– in unworthiness, need, difficulty, etc. – and responds in
mercy and grace, timely help, strength, provision and so
on. When we bless the Lord we review what he is – in his
heavenly and eternal glory, in his revealed attributes, in the
love and grace of his salvation, in his daily works of provi-
dence and care – and we respond point by point, in
wonder, love and praise. This is worship.

Songs that must remain unsung?

But can we use all the psalms? The vast majority, of course,
delight us, and those of us who grew up singing the Psalms
as a regular part of Sunday worship found no difficulty in
adding as a concluding refrain 'Glory be to the Father and
to the Son and to the Holy Spirit', for the sentiments we
expressed in song matched the New Testament revelation
of God in Christ.

But what about:

> If only you would slay the wicked, O God!
> . . . Do I not hate those who hate you . . .?
> I have nothing but hatred for them;
>   I count them my enemies (139:19–22) ?

Or, 'Let death take my enemies by surprise; let them go
down alive to the grave' (55:15)?

About twenty-four psalms contain passages like these
and make us wonder why they are in the Bible at all, in
what sense they can be 'the word of God', and if we should
be expected to use them.

Many commentators take an easy way out. They describe
these 'offending' passages as 'Old Testament morality'
which has now been left behind by the superior revelation
of God in Christ. But this will not do, for in the New
Testament, indeed on the lips of Jesus, we find, 'Woe to
you, teachers of the law and Pharisees, you hypocrites! . . .
You snakes! You brood of vipers! How will you escape
being condemned to hell?' (Matthew 23:29,33).

We find Paul saying, 'If anybody is preaching to you a

gospel other than what you accepted, let him be eternally condemned!' (Galatians 1:9). Also there is the cry of the saints in heaven, 'How long, Sovereign Lord, . . . until you judge the inhabitants of the earth and avenge our blood?' (Revelation 6:10).

The point must be made that indignation expressed in forceful terms is not confined to the Old Testament. It is an aspect of the whole Bible and of the Lord Jesus himself. But we must take care to note that, in respect of the Old Testament as much as the New, vengefulness in thought or deed is expressly forbidden:

> Do not hate your brother in your heart . . .
> Do not seek revenge or bear a grudge . . .
> $\qquad$ (Leviticus 19:17,18)

> Do not say, 'I'll pay you back for this wrong!'
> Wait for the Lord, and he will deliver you.
> $\qquad$ (Proverbs 20:22)

Romans 12:19 and Deuteronomy 32:35 bind the two Testaments together on this topic.

We begin to see some daylight regarding the verses which at first sight offend us when we notice that they are all prayers. We misread them if we see them as evidence of a vengeful spirit, or if we understand them as setting out a programme for human action. On the contrary they are an exercise of committing the problem to the Lord and leaving it there. Far from backing away from these verses in the Psalms, we, who belong to an age that hastens to take vengeance and to solve its problems with bombs, should rather admire and desire that spirit which flew to prayer and left it at that.

There remains, of course, the vigorous way in which the prayers were phrased. Here is an example that startles us by its plain speaking and at the same time illustrates why the psalmists felt that they could pray as they did:

> Appoint an evil man to oppose him;
>> let an accuser stand at his right hand.
> When he is tried, let him be found guilty
>> (Psalm 109:6–7).

In this psalm David is enduring false, malicious accusation. Now, according to God's law in Deuteronomy 19:16–19, the punishment of a false witness is to suffer what he would have inflicted. Possibly, were we placed in a Psalm 109 situation, we would cry out 'Lord, please deal with this trouble!' and leave it at that. But because God is unchanging, he will answer that prayer by bringing on the accusers what they would have done to us! That is his way.

In other words, where we would pray *blandly*, the Psalms pray *realistically*, facing up to the implications of what they are asking.

We need to stop backing off from these bits of the psalms which, initially, are difficult to take. Most of them arise, like Psalm 109, from Deuteronomy 19:16–19. God's legal principle is that the wrongful accuser will receive what he wrongly planned to inflict. That is what God is like. That is the way he runs his world.

Our problem is put in a nutshell by Psalm 143:11,12. We would find no difficulty in praying verse 11: 'For your name's sake, O Lord, preserve my life.' But what about verse 12?: 'In your unfailing love, silence [*i.e.* in death] my enemies.'

Surely it is worth wondering if our unease arises from an absence of *holy* anger and *righteous* moral outrage in our make-up? The fact that possibly we may not be able to pray such prayers without a sinful, vengeful spirit creeping in, is not to say that no-one can! Certainly it is much, much nearer the truth to say that the psalmists who could and did pray in this way were ahead of us in holiness, than to dismiss their prayers as evidence of a lower morality.

Do the Psalms point to the Lord Jesus Christ?

From a very early point in Old Testament times there was a longing for a king. This is reflected in Judges 17:6: 'In those days Israel had no king; everyone did as he saw fit'. (*cf.* Judges 18:1).

The assumption behind these verses is that 'if only we had a king, all this religious heresy (Judges 17), social unrest (Judges 18), and moral corruption Judges 19ff.), would be dealt with: things would be just perfect.' But, of course, when they did get a king they found that they had to rephrase their hopes! They had to begin to say, 'If only we had a *perfect* king . . .!'

But such a person was not to be found. In the books of Kings the spotlight swings to and fro from the ordered succession of Davidic kings in the south, to the quickly changing kings of the north. But they were all alike, failures personally and politically, and the perfect king bringing the perfect society remained an unfulfilled hope.

But hope sprang out of disappointment and developed in intensity. The Psalms reflect it as they sing of a king who faces world opposition (2:1–3; 110:1ff.), but is victorious (45:3–5; 89:22,23). By the Lord's help (18:46–50; 21:1–13) he establishes world rule (2:8–12; 45:17; 72:8–11; 110:5, 6), based on Zion (2:6), marked by righteousness (45:4,6,7; 72:2,3; 101:1–8). His rule is everlasting (21:4; 45:6; 72:5), peaceful (72:7), prosperous (72:16) and devoted (72:5). The king is pre-eminent among people (45:2,7), friend of the poor and enemy of the oppressor (72:2–4,12–14). He owns an everlasting name (72:17) and enjoys everlasting blessing (45:2). He is heir to David's covenant (89:28–37; 132:11,12) and to Melchizedek's priesthood (110:4). He belongs to the Lord (89:18), is his Son (2:7; 89:27), sits at his right hand (110:1) and is himself divine (45:6).

It is very likely that these psalms were used as 'Coronation anthems', sung before the new king as he took his throne, in order to 'hold him to the highest'. But the reality was always more than any mere son of David could be. It

awaited the unique Son of David who is also the Son of God
(Luke 1:32).

A main lesson: take it to the Lord

Psalms is the longest book in the Bible. It is gloriously
varied in style, subjects, thoughts, poetic expression and
literary form. Surely it is a bit ambitious to ask if there is
one line of thought that runs through it all! If anything can
make a bid to be such a single line of thought it is this:
Take it to the Lord in prayer.

We meet people in sickness (88:15), persecution
(143:11,12), loneliness (142:4), joy (145:1,21) and so on.
But they have this in common, that they are determined to
bring all of life to the Lord in committed, urgent prayer.
Surrounded by troubles, they stop to remember him, how
great he is, the wonders he has done (78:9–11; 74:12–17;
77:7–12). They know how meaningful and essential it is to
give up listening to themselves and their troubles, and to
start talking to themselves about a great, sovereign, loving
and unforgetting God. He is a God who will prove to be
sufficient as they lean upon him in the present (23,121)
and whose promises guarantee a future where all will be
well (96:11–13).

> **A Scenic Route Through
> Old Testament Worship: The Psalms**
> _____
> Meet the congregations of the Old Testament church as
> they brought their prayers and praises to God

Four weeks of short daily Bible readings with brief notes

Week 1: Some favourite psalms:
A taste of a wonderful part of the Bible

Day 1. Read Psalm 8. The majestic Lord

Here is something typical of the Psalms: everything starts with God, not with the world around or with people. The Psalms are God-centred and here is his greatness in relation to earth and the heavens (verse 1); his greatness as Creator (verse 3) and as the one who orders life on earth (verses 6–8), giving man and beast their respective places in the scheme of things. The *name* of the Lord (verses 1,9) is shorthand for all that he has revealed to be true about himself. 'Majestic' puts him at the pinnacle of the power-structure; as to *glory* (verse 1), his is higher than the highest we know; as to power (verse 3), his fingers are sufficient to position moon and stars! Yet he (literally) 'remembers' and 'visits' us (verse 4).

Day 2. Read Psalm 23. The Shepherd and his sheep

Every aspect of life comes in this brief Psalm: verse 2, rest and activity; verse 3, the inward soul and the outward path; verses 4–5, life's troubles and life's happiness; verse 5, hospitality and hostility; verses 5–6, present and future. And all this varied life is lived within the Shepherd's care, where the sheep is at rest and in safety. See how the *he* of verses 2 and 3 becomes the more directly personal *you* of verse 4, and how the shepherd who leads ahead (verse 2), becomes the guardian alongside (verse 4) – for the deeper the darkness, the closer the presence. His protection surrounds us, as he goes before (verse 2), walks alongside (verse 4) and, in *goodness and love*, follows behind (verse 6). The chief virtue of a sheep is to relax, rest, and leave it to the Shepherd.

Day 3. Read Psalm 46. Present help

This psalm is all *about* God until suddenly (verse 10) he speaks for himself: 'Relax ... I am God.' Circumstances (verses 2,3) were hostile, waters roaring; people (verse 6) were hostile, nations roaring, but the Lord said 'Relax ... I am God.' As our *refuge* (verse 1) we can run to him; as *with us* (verses 7,11) he has come to us; as *strength* and *help* he is enough for each day's need (verse 1); as *fortress* (verses 7,11), literally, 'top-security', he lifts us out of reach of threat. So 'Relax ... I am God.'

Day 4. Read Psalm 84. To be a pilgrim

The Psalms reveal God's people enjoying his presence everywhere, yet there was one special place of his presence for Old Testament people, his dwelling-place (verse 1), the Jerusalem Temple. To be there was the great object of heart-longing. To be there was a special blessing. In the birds flying and nesting in the temple the psalmist saw a parable; what a place of safety it was! Even though there was a constantly burning fire on the altar a bird could safely nest, and so might each and all of his people find peace with God there. No wonder then that the pilgrimage (verses 5,6), though demanding, was gladly endured. The envisaged benefits (verses 10–12) more than compensated – the sunlight and shelter of his presence and his grace and glory (favour and honour) awaiting the pilgrim walker (verse 11).

Day 5. Read Psalm 95. Worshipping and listening

This psalm is in three parts: (a) Verses 1–5, an invitation followed by an explanation: we are called to worship because of what the Lord is, *great*, *a great King*, sovereign over every aspect of the world. (b) Verses 6–7a, an invitation followed by an explanation: we are called to worship because of what we are, his *people*, his *flock*. (c) Verses 7b–11, the place of singing and bowing in worship is also the place of listening to the Lord's word, so as to embark on a life of trust. Meribah and Massah were two names for a waterless place on the road from Egypt (see Exodus 17) where the people grumbled in doubt rather than trusting in faith that the Lord would provide. He loves to be worshipped, heard and trusted.

Day 6. Read Psalm 103. The father with a mother's love

This title for Psalm 103 expresses what verse 13 says: 'Like as a father has a mother's love for his children' – 'Like as a mother comforts her darling, answers his crying with kind, loving tone, folds in her arms and carries and soothes him, so the Lord loves and comforts his own.' Look up Isaiah 49:15. But love cannot be seen as love until it does something for the loved one: how deeply do we prize the Lord's forgiveness (verse 3), redemption (verse 4), renewing strength (verse 5), his all-covering love (verse 11), his eternal love (verse 17)?

Day 7. Read Psalm 145. Great . . . gracious . . . righteous

The psalm is built around these words in, verses 3,8,17, but what a wonderful collection of the attributes of God the whole psalm is: power (verses 4–6,12); tender goodness (verses 7,9); caring and provident (verses 14–16); and (almost the most precious of all) 'near' (verse 18), for the word contains the idea of the 'next of kin' – the one who, in the Old Testament, freely shoulders our burdens, meets our needs, makes our wants his own. Rightly the psalm is one of first person singular response (verses 1–2,21).

Week 2: Psalms in the life of David

Day 1. Read Psalm 59. Getting on top of things. (Background: 1 Samuel 19:9–17)

David was on the run from Saul's hit men. The story in Samuel only tells the beginning and end of the incident. The psalm reveals the daily and nightly pressure under which David lived. How did he rise above it? (a) He prayed (verses 1–5): the first move in times of pressure is to 'take it to the Lord in prayer'; (b) He trusted (verses 9–10), watching not for his enemies to attack, but for God to come to his aid; (c) He found security in God: in verses 1,9,16,17 *protect* and *fortress* express the idea of 'top-security', a lifting up (inaccessibly) above the threat. How surprised the watching hit men must have been to hear David and Michal singing and making music to God while still in the thick of their trouble (verses 16,17)!

Day 2. Read Psalm 57. Where the real shelter is. (Background: 1 Samuel 22:1)

Humanly speaking, how cornered David must have felt – a fugitive from Saul, sneaking into a cave for shelter (see title): the cold stone of the rock around and overhead, the menacing beasts outside (verse 4)! But bring together the words in the title 'in the cave' and the words in verse 1 *in the shadow of your wings*. As David looked at the overshadowing cave walls, it was not stone he saw, but the sheltering, comforting wings of his God, brooding over and around him like a great mother bird. Isn't this a real 'practising of the presence of God'? – not in the sense of trying to force ourselves to feel he is with us, but in the deeper sense of resting on his promise that he will never leave us (Hebrews 13:5,6).

Day 3. Read Psalm 51:1–6. The power of repentance. (Background 2 Samuel 11 – 12)

The most important word in these verses is the *for* at the beginning of verse 3. It explains how all the benefits of verses 1 and 2 can be experienced. In David there is 'transgression, iniquity, sin', but in the Lord there is 'mercy, love, compassion', whereby sin can be 'blotted out, washed away, cleansed'. But the clue to the experience of forgiveness is acknowledging that I am a sinner – just that! (verses 3,4). David does not specify his particular sins of adultery and murder at this time because what he says is true of all sins. It could not be put better than 2 Samuel 12:13.

Day 4. Read Psalm 51:7–19. The prayer of the penitent

David's prayer touches on four topics and becomes a model prayer for us as we too repent before God: (a) To be accepted before God (verses 7–9): our sins offend him and need to be blotted out; (b) To be rid of sin (verses 10–12): true repentance must be accompanied by a real desire to become a different person; (c) To tell others about this praiseworthy God (verses 13–15); (d) To ask God to put right all the harm our sin has done to others (verses 16–19). David was king and knew rightly that his sin was destructive of his kingdom. But the same is true of us in the Body of Christ. We never sin, however privately, without hurting the Body.

Day 5. Read Psalm 3. Peace in time of stress. (Background: 2 Samuel 15 – 17)

When his eldest surviving son rebelled against him, David made a strategic withdrawal eastwards from Jerusalem, over the Kidron and the north slopes of Olives to Bahurim, then across Jordan and north thirty miles to Mahanaim. This psalm is the product of the first night on that weary road, when God visited him with a surprising peace and a good night's sleep (verses 5,6). How did such calm come to him? (a) By seeing that God is sufficient even for this emergency (verses 1–3); (b) By discovering that prayer brings peace and real assurance about the future (verses 4–8). First he turns to God and then, in answer to prayer, receives from God an experience of rest (Philippians 4:6,7), and finally goes forward with God into the threatening future.

Day 6. Read Psalm 63. Thirsty – but for God. (Background: 2 Samuel 15 – 17)

The second night of the flight from Absalom, but this time sleep eludes David (verse 6). Yet his thoughts (marvellously!) are not self-pitying; rather the wearying, waterless terrain through which he has marched that day becomes a picture of a dry soul longing for God (verse 1). This

71

longing finds expression in remembering and praising (verses 2–6), joy in divine help (verses 7,8), trust for the future (verses 9–11). Note the spirit of determination all the way through – 'I seek' (verse 1); 'I will praise' (verses 4,5); 'I remember . . . meditate' (verse 6); 'I sing' (verse 7); 'I stay close' (verse 8, literally 'My soul follows you closely'.)

Day 7. Read Psalm 30. Out of the depths.
(Background: 2 Samuel 5:6–13)
If the 'house' (not 'temple' as NIV) in the heading is David's own house, then we learn that as he planned to 'move in' he was visited by a potentially terminal illness (verses 6–10). Certainly the passage in 2 Samuel breathes a complacently confident spirit that the world was now at David's feet! The perils of a day of prosperity are greater than those of a day of difficulty. He needed the shock realization of his fragility to bring him to his spiritual senses – his total dependence in prayer (verses 1–3), a true understanding of his experience (verses 6–7) – with resultant joy and thanksgiving (verses 11,12).

Week 3: Facing life

Day 1. Read Psalm 1. The key to all life
(a) *Commitment* (verse 1): Alter the translation to 'has determined not to walk . . . stand . . . sit'; (b) *Contrast* (verse 2): a very different foundation for life – not the 'council of the wicked' but the *law* (*i.e.* 'teaching') of the Lord, capturing our hearts (*delight*) and our minds (*meditates*); (c) *Consequence* (verse 3): The Hebrew suggests 'and consequently he is like . . .'; *planted* is literally 'transplanted'. Dwelling on God's word brings us into a new position where life is refreshed by streams of water and bears fruit. After *prospers* (verse 3) imagine the words 'in the Lord's time', for the psalmist is too wise to think that prosperity is automatic! (d) *Condemnation* (verses 4,5); (e) *Confidence* (verse 6): ever in his care.

Day 2. Read Psalm 37:1–11. Facing adversity

There is nothing out of date about the problem of seeing people who never think of God prospering and reaching positions of influence, while those who are devoted to him are busy getting nowhere, seeing none of their hopes fulfilled (verse 4), possibly under a cloud of false accusation (verse 6) – no sign of the meek inheriting the earth (verse 11)! In this life things are all too often far from ideal, very unfair, and unjust too! The reply of the psalm sounds simplistic, but is simply effective. It is the life of trust and commitment, patience, personal restraint and trustful expectation. In a word, the God-centred life.

Day 3. Read Psalm 42. Depression

Talking to oneself, they say, is the first sign of madness. Maybe. But giving oneself a good talking to is one of the signs of spiritual health. This is exactly what this psalm is doing. Since the psalmist is fondly recalling temple festivals (verse 4), but now hears the thunder of waterfalls in Hermon (verses 6–7), and is surrounded by mockers (verses 3,10), we must imagine an exile from his Jerusalem home – tearful (verse 3), oppressed (verse 7), and suffering (verse 10). What a recipe for depression! He *is* downcast (verses 5,11), but he is not lying down under it, grumbling, self-pitying, 'chewing the fat'. He is directive with himself, determined to bring God into his life (verse 6), and frank with God about his problems (verse 7). Above all, he maintains a sure hope (verses 5,11).

Day 4. Read Psalm 49. Earthly inequalities, heavenly benefits

He is a confident chap, this psalmist! There is a problem but he has a solution (verses 1–4). The problem is *wicked deceivers* (verse 5) who are doing very nicely, thank you (verses 16,18). So had he, or a friend, just lost out to a crooked finance company? That's the sort of situation in any case. What, then, is the solution to facing a life which contains all too much of this sort of thing? Think about death and the life to come. *They* have no hopeful expectation in death (verses 13,14); but for us, on the contrary, after death all present inequalities will be corrected (verse 14) and redemption awaits (verse 15), not captives of the grave but 'taken' by the Lord to himself (Genesis 5:24).

Day 5. Read Psalm 73. God is my portion

This psalm continues the thought of Psalm 49. Faith says how good God is but life often seems to contradict this (verses 1–3). Those who are spiritually careless prosper, while the devoted person has trouble on trouble (verses 4–14). But wait! Think in terms of eternal destiny (verse 17). The contrast between verses 18–20 and 23–25 could not be more complete. What richness is here! – to experience God's presence and his holding hand, his plan over all our life and experiences, and *afterwards . . . glory* (verses 23–24). It is only those who are sure about heaven who have the strength and insight to manage life on earth.

Day 6. Read Psalm 107:1–22. The lifeline of prayer

Here is as good a collection of the different experiences of God's people as we will easily find. The first 'some' (verses 4,5) experienced privation and hostile circumstances; the second 'some' (verses 10,11) brought themselves into bondage by flouting God's will; the third 'some' (verses 17,18) made their lives miserable by rebellious, unruly ways. But they all had this in common: they met life's difficulties head on in prayer (verses 6,13,19) and experienced the Lord's sufficient answers (verses 7,14,20). Psalm 65:2 has a lovely title for the Lord: 'O you who hear prayer'.

Day 7. Read Psalm 139. No escape . . . no regrets

Verses 7–12 review a variety of possible 'escapes' from God, not because the psalmist wants to get away from him, but because he needs the comfort of reminding himself that he cannot. He wrote in a time of distress: there were people around him whose only desire was to speak ill of the Lord (verses 19–22). The strength of his reaction to them reveals the depth of his horror at what they represented and of the hurt they gave him. But in this shadow hanging over his life he had a secure refuge in God, from whom there was no escape: this wonderful God knew all about him (verses 1–4), hemmed him in, not restrictively, but protectively, and sheltered him with his own hand (verse 5). God was present with him in every place (verses 7–12). From such a safe place in God, life can be faced.

Week 4: The individual and the world. Two prominent themes in Psalms

Day 1. Read Psalm 119:25–32. Time of trouble, time of . . .?

'I, me, my' come in every line of this reading, typical of the very personal religion of the Psalms; typically too, the individual is in trouble! How do we react to a time of trouble? The writer of this psalm reacted: (a) By making it a time of prayer. Seven out of the eight verses of this section are prayers – more than in any other part of Psalm 119; (b) by recognizing it as a time of temptation (verses 28–29), a special request to be kept from taking false paths; (c) by making it a time of commitment – to meditate on God's word, choose his way, hold fast, and make a special effort (verses 27,30–32).

Day 2. Read Psalm 27. Light and salvation

Again 'I, me, my' come in every verse (except 14, which is probably David giving an order to himself). It says: (a) My security is in the Lord (verses 1–3); (b) my longing is for the Lord (verses 4–6); (c) my confidence is in the Lord whose devotion to me is more certain than (even) parental love (verses 7–10); (d) my future rests with the Lord who will lead, protect, and bring me through (verses 11–13). Therefore (verse 14) he takes himself in hand and tells himself what to do (see Week 3, Day 3).

Day 3. Read Psalm 121. Sixfold keeping

In NIV, 'watch over' (verses 3,4,5,7,8) is the same verb that is translated 'keep' in verse 7. So it comes six times in the psalm – a psalm of our sixfold security in the Lord's care. Whatever the threat was – maybe we are not told in order that we can slot our own problem in! – the psalm says that the answer lies in the great Creator God who keeps each of his people, and all his people (verses 1–4). He keeps us sheltered from real dangers (like sunstroke), and imaginary ones (like moonstroke), in a round-the-clock vigil (verses 5–6). He keeps us from all harm for all time, beginning now (verses 7–8). Verse 3 shows how detailed his care is; verse 5, how personal, interposing himself between us and the threat; and verses 7 and 8, how total.

Day 4. Read Psalm 116:1–14. Personal prayer, personal commitment

This psalm, too, originated in a time of trouble which became the occasion of prayer (verses 3,4). This is not as easy as it sounds. In our experience the time of trouble is so often the time when it is hardest to pray, even though, by failing to pray, we cut ourselves off from our surest comfort and help. The experience of answered prayer led the psalmist to a deeper love for the Lord (verses 1,2), a clearer knowledge of God's gracious character (verses 5,6), and a definite personal commitment to respond to the Lord in daily life (verses 9,12). The order of verses 13 and 14 is important. Always, our first response is to take what the Lord freely gives; only then can we take up the task of living out the godly life in the fellowship of his people.

Day 5. Read Psalm 2. King of Zion . . . King of the world

The Psalms have a clear vision for the world – of a great, divine King reigning over the whole world from Zion. The Lord promised David a continuing line of kings (2 Samuel 7:16), but at some point this developed into the expectation of a special son of David who would also be Son of God and who would reign for ever. Think, then, of Psalm 2 as a coronation song, composed for the day when one of the Davidic kings ascended the throne. Would he be the promised Messiah? The vision of the ideal is held up before him: this is what he should be – the 'son' (verse 7), the world's king (verse 8), and the one in whom any and all can find refuge (verse 12). We are privileged to belong to that Zion (Hebrews 12:22–24), and to live under that King (Luke 1:30–33).

Day 6. *Read Psalm 96. When the Lord comes to reign*
Parallel with the expectation of the perfect King was the expectation that it would be the Lord himself who would come to reign. Already his people know him as the great King (Psalm 95:3; 96:4) and have the duty to make him known worldwide (verse 10). But when he does come to reign, all creation will be 'set to rights' (verses 11–13) – a good translation of 'judge' in verse 13. God the Creator will not desert his creation or allow the damage and corruption brought by sin (Genesis 3:18) to have the last word. He will come. He will reign, and there will be a new heaven and a new earth (Isaiah 11:6–9; 65:17–25; Revelation 21:1–5).

Day 7. *Read Psalm 100. The Lord's worldwide people*
'From earth's wide bounds, from ocean's farthest coast, through gates of pearl stream in the countless host, singing to Father, Son and Holy Ghost: Hallelujah.' The hymn finds its fulfilment in Revelation 7:9–10 but its inspiration in Psalm 100. This lovely psalm is a threefold call twice repeated (verses 1,2, 'Shout, Worship, Come'; verse 4, 'Enter, Give thanks, Praise'), followed each time by an explanation (verse 3, 'The Lord is God'; verse 5, 'The Lord is good'). Because he is God we are safe in his care (verse 3); because he is good, we experience his unchanging, faithful love (verse 5).

4

The Voice of Prophecy

In their own day the prophets were headline-makers and pace-setters in the national news. So, if we find their books tedious, unclear, less than exciting, the fault does not lie with them!

Isaiah drew a taunting response from the political leaders of his day – a sure sign, then as now, that his message had hit home (Isaiah 28:9,10)! Jeremiah was flogged and tortured (Jeremiah 20:2) and set upon by a lynch mob (Jeremiah 26:7–11). Amos had a deportation order served on him because his message was a nationwide talking point (Amos 7:10,12,13).

It is all very different from our reaction to the three long books and the thirteen shorter books of the prophets which we find in our Old Testament!

How ordinary they were!

In one way there was nothing special about the prophets. Those who have left personal testimonies reveal themselves as people with an experience of God with which we can all identify. The form their experience took was, of course, individual to them, as indeed ours is, but at heart they were the same as we: chosen, forgiven, regenerate, and called.

Isaiah met God in the experience of the forgiveness of sins: 'See, this has touched your lips; your guilt is taken away and your sin atoned for' (Isaiah 6:7). The sudden awareness of how holy God is made him realize how serious was his sinfulness (Isaiah 6:3,5), but his cry of despair was at once met by a divine response bringing the assurance that his sin had been atoned for, covered by an exactly matching price.

Jeremiah was different. He felt totally inadequate to be a prophet and the Lord came to him with the assurance he needed:

> Before I formed you in the womb I knew you,
> before you were born I set you apart;
> I appointed you as a prophet (Jeremiah 1:5).

In a word, whatever Jeremiah felt about himself and his lack of ability, it was in fact for this very work that the Lord had him in mind even before he was conceived; between conception and birth he was set apart to be God's man for God's work. Consequently he is a prophet, not because he felt able for it, nor by personal decision, but by divine appointment. God had chosen, set apart, and predestined Jeremiah for this vocation.

Ezekiel, the prophet who has left us the longest account of his call, was different again: 'As he spoke, the Spirit came into me and raised me to my feet, and I heard him speaking to me' (Ezekiel 2:2). Totally overawed by the vision of God which had been granted to him (Ezekiel 1, see especially verse 28), Ezekiel was indwelt by the Holy Spirit and lifted up by him to stand before God to hear his word.

Amos is the fourth prophet who has left us an account of his call. The heart of his testimony is this: 'I was neither a prophet nor a prophet's son, but I was a shepherd, and I also took care of sycamore-fig trees. But the Lord took me . . . and said to me: "Go, prophesy to my people . . ."' (Amos 7:14,15).

He was not a prophet by profession, nor by training ('prophet's son', *cf.* 2 Kings 6:1, literally, not 'company' but 'sons'). Rather the call of God intruded into his farming life and sent him to the new work of 'prophesying', to minister the Lord's word to the Lord's people.

What then is so unusual about all this? Do we not see ourselves and our spiritual experience reflected in these brothers of old?

Like Jeremiah, we too have our place in the eternal plans of God who 'chose us in him [the Lord Jesus Christ] before the creation of the world' (Ephesians 1:4).

Like Isaiah, we have been brought into God's presence and fellowship by atonement: 'In him [the Lord Jesus Christ] we have redemption through his blood, the forgiveness of sins' (Ephesians 1:7).

Like Ezekiel, the Holy Spirit has come to live in us too: 'Do you not know that your body is a temple of the Holy Spirit, who is in you, whom you have received from God?' (1 Corinthians 6:19).

Like Amos (along with Isaiah, Jeremiah, Ezekiel and all the Lord's prophet-people) we are called to the task of bearing witness: 'You will be my witnesses' (Acts 1:8); 'On my servants ... I will pour out my Spirit ... and they will prophesy' (Acts 2:18).

But alongside these basic ways in which we can identify with the prophets, there were about them things that were unique, special God-given abilities which were theirs alone.

Inspiration

While we bear witness to the word of God, they actually spoke it! It is put very crisply at the beginning of the book of Amos: 'The words of Amos ... This is what the Lord says' (Amos 1:1,3).

This means exactly what it says. While Amos spoke words that 'came naturally' to him – using his own ordinary vocabulary, speaking with his own accent, 'doing his own thing' – the Lord was speaking *his* words, saying what *he* wanted to say, 'doing *his* thing!'

It was the same for Jeremiah: 'The Lord reached out his hand and touched my mouth and said to me ... Now I have put my words in your mouth' (Jeremiah 1:9).

Typically of his imaginative ways, Ezekiel tells how the Lord gave him a written scroll and obliged him to eat it (Ezekiel 2:8 – 3:3)! Every detail of this incident is important but just notice how it begins and where it ends. It began with a command: 'You must speak my words to them' (Ezekiel 2:7). Note the plural, 'words'. Ezekiel's job is not to pass on the 'drift' or general idea of the mind of God, but to speak in such a way that people would hear God's *words*.

How could this be? How can a human mind think out God's truth and a human tongue express it in God's words? Only by a special, unique work of God which the Bible claims but never explains. This is why Ezekiel can only help us by an illustration – as if the words of God were written out and he ate the book! Yet the experience was real and effective for, having eaten the scroll, Ezekiel receives the repeated command: 'Son of man, go now to the house of Israel and speak my words to them' (Ezekiel 3:4).

This, of course, is a mystery to us. It is a mystery because the Bible never explains how verbal inspiration happens. English translations have made us familiar with the expression 'The word of the Lord came to ...' (*e.g.* 1 Kings 17:2,8), but the Hebrew which is translated in this way simply says 'the word of the Lord *was* to ...', meaning 'became a personal, living reality to ...'. How it did so we are not told; it is simply affirmed that it was so.

Living in God's fellowship

We are helped a little to understand when Jeremiah says, of false prophets, that they had never been members of 'the council of the Lord':

> 'Which of them has stood in the council of the
> Lord
> to see or to hear his word? ...
> If they had stood in my council, they would have
> proclaimed my words ...' (Jeremiah 23:18,22).

Amos applies the same truth to the true prophet: 'The Sovereign Lord does nothing without revealing his plan [opening his council] to his servants the prophets' (Amos 3:7).

The key word here can mean 'council' in the sense of a group (Psalm 89:7); it can also mean 'counsel', the advice given, or decision reached by such an assembly (Psalm 64:2, 'conspiracy'); and it can mean 'fellowship', the close relationship enjoyed by those who share each other's company (Psalm 55:14). The prophet is a living person brought near to God.

In this way the Old Testament pictures God's decisions as made in a 'council meeting' (1 Kings 22:19,20). The prophet is admitted into this 'council' to share the 'fellowship' of the Lord and to learn his 'counsel', his heavenly decisions. It is in this setting that the unique inspiration of the prophet takes place.

Tape-recorders or persons

When we wonder how a mere human could actually speak the words of God, it is all too easy to think of tape-recorders, as if the Lord used the prophets as machines, overriding their personality, feeding into them thoughts and words which they might not have chosen. Yet how very far this is from what we find in their books! They are all so personally distinctive! They put things in their own individual ways: the majestic poetry of Isaiah or Zephaniah; the pedestrian, hesitating style of Jeremiah; the complex, imaginative acts of Ezekiel; or the homely talks of Malachi. They have not been forced into anyone else's mould; their personalities shine through, even larger than life.

We must think therefore along a different line. Mankind was made in the image of God (Genesis 1:27). As Genesis 3 – 4 and the rest of the Bible and our own experience of ourselves and the world show, when the image of God in humankind was marred and corrupted by sin, inhumanity crept in. Adam ceased to see Eve as his glorious counterpart (Genesis 2:23), and began to see and treat her as a baby factory (Genesis 3:20). Cain murdered Abel (Genesis 4:8), and the world became full of menace and vengeful violence (Genesis 4:13,23,24). By contrast, the saving work of the Lord Jesus Christ is defined as bringing about both 'the new man' and 'the likeness of God' (Ephesians 4:20–24).

In the light of all this we can state a principle: the nearer to God we get, the more truly human we become. The more we become like him, the more we become our true selves.

The prophets were brought into such closeness to the Lord, that not only were they more truly human and individual in consequence, but they were enabled in this closeness of fellowship to learn and to become the vehicles of his pure, untarnished word of truth.

The prophet at work

For the most part the prophets communicated the Lord's word by speaking. Jeremiah 7:2 is typical: 'Stand at the gate of the Lord's house and there proclaim this message.'

But on many occasions prophets added to their spoken word by embodying their message in a telling act. Here is Jeremiah again (Jeremiah 19:1,2): 'Buy a clay jar from a potter. Take along some of the elders of the people. . . and go out to . . . the entrance of the Potsherd Gate . . . .'

Jeremiah's message at this point was one of total devastation (Jeremiah 19:3–9). When he had spoken his word, he hurled the earthenware jar he was holding to the ground so that it was smashed, its pieces were scattered and lost among the broken pots dumped at the 'Potsherd Gate', and there was no possibility of anyone ever assembling them again. This act was accompanied by a word: 'I will smash this nation . . . just as this potter's jar is smashed and cannot be repaired' (19:11).

What a 'visual aid!' But it was more than that: it was a separate 'embodiment' of the word of the Lord. It did of course make the message plainer to those present, for what they heard they also saw. But the deeper purpose of the 'telling act' was to send out the ever-effective word of the Lord (Isaiah 55:11) along twin-tracks: the spoken word and the visible word – in the same way that today baptism and the Lord's Supper are visible embodiments of the promises of God in Christ Jesus.

The books of the prophets

In the books of the prophets we have the word as they recorded it for the future.

Amos' great sermon on current affairs (Amos 1:2 – 2:16) could not be preached just as it stands. It is all over too quickly! The minds of the hearers could not travel as fast as that, for all of us are like the man who said to his minister: 'You must speak more slowly, I am a slow listener!' In the same way we can imagine Amos using 1:2 – 2:16 as sermon notes, but giving his congregation plenty of time to let their minds dwell on what he was saying – pausing, developing, saying the same things twice or three times – all the ways in which a careful teacher-preacher tries to bring his hearers along with him.

But afterwards, at home, knowing that what he had said was not just 'the word of man' but also 'the word of God in the words of God', Amos would store away the distilled essence, the carefully prepared written record of the divine message.

Publicizing and preserving

There may be something else. Isaiah was commanded to 'Take a large scroll ['placard'] and write on it with an ordinary pen' (Isaiah 8:1), and on another occasion 'Write it on a tablet . . .' (Isaiah 30:8).

The idea of a 'wall newspaper' springs to mind. Most of the material in the prophets occurs in 'bite-sized chunks' which could, very easily and manageably, be written up publicly. Might we paraphrase Isaiah 8:1 as 'Hire hoarding space?' At any rate, it stands to reason that people who knew that what they said was 'the word of God', would make every effort to give their people the chance to know and study it.

We can well imagine Isaiah with his 'large placard', and share Amos' quiet glee as he pricked the high ecclesiastical pomposity of Amaziah by publishing what passed between them (Amos 7:10–17)!

Be this as it may, it is certain that the prophets were careful curators of the word the Lord had given to them. It is impossible to think that they would either fail to record what had been revealed to them, or would leave the 'words of God' to a version of 'Chinese Whispers' – the reliability of being transmitted by word of mouth depending on the frailty of human memory.

Rather, Jeremiah 36 shows us how their careful records were kept. The faithful Baruch reported: 'He dictated all these words to me, and I wrote them in ink on the scroll' (verse 18).

To Isaiah the Lord commanded: 'Bind up the testimony and seal up the Law ['teaching'] among my disciples' (Isaiah 8:16). In other words, 'Deposit it all for safe keeping with your home-group, the church that meets in your house.'

Whether the individual prophets were directly responsible for the final form of the whole books that bear their names, it is not possible to be sure. There is neither convincing cause to deny that they could have been their own final editors, nor any need to rule out the careful, conserving work of devout disciples.

The prophets' dates

Here is the broad time-line along which the prophets worked:

	700s	600s	500s	400s
760	Amos			
	Jonah			
750	Hosea			
740	Micah			
	Isaiah			
640		Nahum		
		Zephaniah		
620		Jeremiah		
610		Habakkuk		
600			Daniel	
580			Obadiah	
570			Ezekiel	
520			Haggai	
			Zechariah	
430				Malachi

Did you notice that Joel is missing? The reason is that he may be early or late. The indications given in his book are not clear enough to be certain.

In fairness it has to be said that there are those who would propose a much later date for Daniel, and many who would attribute the work of Isaiah to different prophets at different dates. But the point of the chart is that each prophet ministered to his own times and circumstances. It is by listening to what he said then that we can hear what the word of God is saying now.

The prophets' message

Though it is absurd to think of summarizing nearly one-third of the Old Testament in a few paragraphs, there are some characteristic lines of prophetic thought, for the prophets were not innovators but expositors and appliers. It was their task to make existing truth fresh and relevant. Think of it this way:

Holy God: Holy People The God of Moses
One God: World Vision The God of Abraham
Faithful God: Coming King The God of David
Forgiving God: Perfect Saviour The God of the Temple

Moses and the holy God

When Moses met with the Lord at the 'burning bush' (Exodus 3:5), 'God' and 'holiness' were explicitly joined together for the first time. Of course, when we look back into Genesis we see that the Lord is the Holy One, but it is not actually stated that this is so. It is very different from Moses onwards. The work of Moses is dominated by the truth that the Lord is the holy God and all the prophets go on affirming it. Holiness is particularly the message of Isaiah: 'Holy, holy, holy is the Lord Almighty' (Isaiah 6:3).

In order to express a superlative or a special characteristic, Hebrew uses repetition. For example, in 2 Kings 25:15, 'gold or silver' is, literally, 'gold gold ... silver silver', *i.e.* 'the finest gold ... the purest silver'. In Genesis 14:10, 'full of tar pits' is, literally, 'pits pits', *i.e.* 'covered with pits'.

Isaiah 6:3 is the only instance of a quality being stated three times. The Lord is not only 'holy, holy', *i.e.* superlatively and characteristically so, but 'holy, holy, holy', super-superlatively and totally characteristically holy! The Old Testament throughout agrees. It uses 'holy' to describe the Name of the Lord – 'his holy name' – more often than all other adjectives put together. But when we read Isaiah 6:1–8 we learn that this super-superlative holiness is moral holiness before which sinners stand convicted, condemned and lost.

Holy God, holy people

Moses taught that because the Lord is holy, his people must be holy too: 'Be holy, because I, the Lord your God, am holy' (Leviticus 19:2).

This was the whole point of giving the detailed law with its commandments. Each command of the Decalogue, for example, arises from some aspect of the divine nature, so that in his law God is commanding that this or that side of his own character should be obediently lived out by his people.

The seventh commandment is a good illustration of this. The Lord is ever faithful to what he has covenanted, therefore, if his people are to be like him, they too must keep their (marriage) covenant promises and 'not commit adultery' (Exodus 20:14).

The prophets applied the principle of obedience across the board:

(1) To the way people lived. 'Has this house, which bears my Name, become a den of robbers to you?' (Jeremiah 7:11).

A 'robber's den' is a place to which a robber goes for safety and from which he emerges just as much a robber as when he went in! Jeremiah saw people pretending to have a relationship with the Lord, thronging his house, but without any intention of becoming morally and spiritually transformed. They wanted the safety of the Lord's house, so long as it didn't touch the way they lived from Monday to Friday! But the holy God looks for a people growing in holiness.

(2) To the way they worshipped. Isaiah condemned a religion without morality: 'Stop bringing meaningless offerings ... Your hands are full of blood' (Isaiah 1:13–15).

Even the precious rituals of sacrifice, ordained by the Lord himself, are empty in his sight if people think that (as someone said), 'they can pray on their knees on Sunday and on their neighbours for the rest of the week.'

(3) To the way they carried on their business. Amos looked around him at an apparently religious society, but found it to be without righteous social values: 'When will the New Moon be over that we may sell grain? . . . skimping the measure, boosting the price' (Amos 8:5).

The holiness that their religion implied operated when they stood before the Lord, but not when they stood behind their counters!

Abraham: the whole world

We have looked at Moses first because he brought the foundational, early period of revelation to its climax and laid down the basis on which the rest of the Old Testament operates (Genesis 12 – Exodus 40). But the prophets did not forget how the Lord spoke to Abraham and gave his descendants a universal importance: 'All the peoples on earth will be blessed through you' (Genesis 12:3).

No-one encapsulated this better than Isaiah, in the magnificent vision of 25:6–9:

On this mountain the Lord Almighty will prepare
   a feast of rich food for all peoples,
a banquet of aged wine –
   the best of meats and the finest of wines.
On this mountain he will destroy
   the shroud that enfolds all peoples,
the sheet that covers all nations;
   he will swallow up death for ever.
The Sovereign Lord will wipe away the tears
   from all faces;
he will remove the disgrace of his people
   from all the earth . . .
In that day they will say,
'Surely this is our God;
   we trusted in him, and he saved us.'

Of course, there were also other dimensions to the fact of a single, universal God. Amos (1:3 – 2:3) realized that human conscience brought all nations under condemnation before the Judge. All over the world there were people like the Arameans (Amos 1:3–5), or the Philistines (Amos 1:6–8), and the rest. They had never heard the voice of God bringing special revelation as had Israel, but they did have what Paul calls 'the requirements of the law written on their hearts'; they did have a 'conscience . . . bearing witness' (Romans 2:14,15). They needed no other warning that the fearful catalogue of crimes against humanity which Amos recorded against them would make them guilty before the Judge of all the earth.

But Amos, too, has another view of the end, when 'all the nations that bear my name' will live under the rule of the coming David and enjoy messianic prosperity and security (Amos 9:11–15).

David: the messianic king

With the Lord's promises to David (2 Samuel 7), the Old Testament's great hope began to take a royal shape: a king was coming.

In 2 Samuel 7 Nathan promised David a continuing line of kings whose successive reigns would guarantee him an everlasting dynasty. But at some point it became clear that no merely human line of descent could ever produce the perfect king, and the prophets began to voice a full-blown longing for the kingly Messiah. True, he would be of human birth and sit on David's throne: 'The Virgin will be with child and will give birth to a son' (Isaiah 7:14). . . . 'He will reign on David's throne and over his kingdom' (Isaiah 9:7). But he would also be much more: '. . . he will be called Wonderful Counsellor, Mighty God . . .' (Isaiah 9:6).

How the Messiah-King would be both human and divine, the Old Testament does not say. This is part of the messianic enigma awaiting solution at the coming of the Lord Jesus.

The temple: forgiveness, salvation

As we saw, the tabernacle/house/temple was the place where the holy God lived among his people. Special arrangements were therefore required in order that they, sinners that they were, might live with him in peace and safety and enjoy his presence. God's provision for this was the system of sacrifices.

The heart of the meaning of the sacrifices (as we have seen) was experienced on the Day of Atonement: 'The goat will carry on itself all their sins' (Leviticus 16:22). But as that towering genius, Isaiah, pondered this mystery of sin-bearing – how one, by God's merciful design, could stand as the substitute for another – the truth was revealed that in full reality only a *person* can substitute for *persons*. An animal dying can illustrate a truth, but the truth itself requires a person to die, one willing and fit to bear the sins of others. And so it happened: 'He poured out his life unto death, and was numbered with the transgressors. . . . he bore (carried) the sin of many' (Isaiah 53:12).

In these ways the prophets took the great foundational truths which they inherited, applied them afresh to the people around them, and looked forward to the great Day when all would be consummated and, as Joshua said in his day, 'Not one of all the Lord's good promises to the house of Israel failed; every one was fulfilled' (Joshua 21:45).

> **A Scenic Route Through
> The Old Testament Prophets**
> ———————
> **Meet and hear the great preachers of the Old Testament**

Four weeks of short daily Bible readings with brief notes

Week 1: Meet the prophets

*Day 1. Read Hosea 1:1–8; 3:1–2. The voice of God
through a broken heart*
Hosea ministered in the northern Kingdom, Israel, at a
time of great material prosperity but steep decline in true
religion and spirituality. The Lord spoke to him through a
bitter sadness in his own home: the infidelity of his wife –
so we gather from hints dropped. It is only of his first child
that it says she 'bore him' (1:3) and by 3:2 he has to buy her,
presumably as one would a prostitute. 3:1 is the verse to
concentrate on. Hosea's love for Gomer is modelled on the
Lord's love for his people, an undying love for us in our
waywardness, love that reaches out to seek and save and to
bring home.

*Day 2. Read Amos 7:10–17. Resolute prophet . . .
unstoppable word*
A little before Hosea (about 750 BC) Amos too prophesied
to Israel. He got into trouble with 'the establishment'
through denouncing the pursuit of affluence at the
expense of the poor and of spiritual values. Amos was
confident of the call of God (verse 14–15); he knew that
what he was saying was 'what the Lord says' (verse 17); and
that no opposition could stop the word (verses 16,17). All
the prophets were the same. And in our situation, if we are
to 'go public for God', we need to be as confident as Amos
that we are following his call and that we possess and are
determined to share the unstoppable word of God, the
Bible.

Day 3. Read Habakkuk 2:1–4; 3:17–19. Wrestling, waiting, trusting

The prophets were truly human. The confidence with which they proclaimed the word of God when they received it, was often the end product of wrestling to understand just what it was God was doing and planning. Habakkuk had two problems with this we can identify: Why does God seem to do nothing about the wickedness in the world (1:2)?; and why, when he acts, does he use such unworthy agents – in this case the Babylonians (1:5, 6, 13)? The answer the Lord gave him and his response to it will do for us too: hold to what the Lord has spoken (2:2), wait for his word to be fulfilled (2:3) and trust him, come what may (2:4; 3:17–19).

Day 4. Read Jonah 1:1–3; 3:1–3. Second chance

What a very human prophet was Jonah! Unlike Isaiah with his prompt 'Send me', Jonah rather replied 'What! Me?', and promptly set off in the opposite direction. Did the Lord then give up on Jonah and look for someone else? Certainly not! He does not give us up; he pursues us to bring us back into his will; he gives the second chance (3:1). Somehow in God's way of doing things, only Jonah will do as a prophet to Nineveh. This is the serious importance of the individual in the plan of God. There is no such thing as 'Here I am, send him/her'. Each holds a key place no-one else can fill.

Day 5. Read Jeremiah 1:4–9. Not an afterthought

Jeremiah did not run away but, like Jonah, he did say 'What! Me?' (verse 6), through a sense of inability ('I do not know how') and immaturity ('only a child'). The Lord met him with three assurances: (a) He had long since prepared Jeremiah for all this (verse 5; compare Ephesians 1:4; 2:10); (b) he would keep Jeremiah company all through the hard slog of obedience (verse 8); and (c) he gave him the words to say (verse 9), with the assurance that he would make his word effective (verse 12). Jeremiah's book shows that the prophet never did stop trembling, nor lose his sense of inadequacy. But neither did he let his feelings stop him from obeying.

Day 6. Read Ezekiel 1:1–3, 28; 2:1–4. The great God of the prophets

The 'thirtieth year' (verse 1) may be Ezekiel's age – the time when, as a priest (verse 3), he would in other circumstances have begun his priestly service. But he was a captive exile in Babylon! On this day of disappointed hopes he was granted 'visions of God' (verse 1), and a sense of the hand of God on his life (verse 3). The Lord is never defeated by our circumstances or our disappointments. Amongst all else the vision was one of surrounding divine mercy and care: for the rainbow is the sign of God's protective promises (verse 28; Genesis 9:13–16). Great as was the God whom Ezekiel saw in vision, he intended that this man should come into his fellowship and hear his word (2:1,2). The prophets were unique, but for us too God is caring, undefeated, opening his fellowship, sharing his word.

Day 7. Read Haggai 1:1–7. Speaking for God in the day of inflation

The exile was over and the people back from Babylon. It was a time of prosperity and comfort, living in 'panelled houses' (verse 4), the equivalent of cavity-wall insulation; pretty luxurious. But for all their expenditure on self it was hard to make ends meet. The economy was depressed, they weren't really satisfied, and the money seemed to go nowhere (verse 6). But, without a house, how could the Lord come to live among them – that's what the house meant! They thought they could manage just as well without his indwelling presence!

Week 2: The prophets' word and message

Day 1. Read Ezekiel 2:7 – 3:4. The actual words of God

What the Lord asked was surely impossible – to 'speak my words' (2:7)? Note the plural – not just the general idea of what the Lord wanted to be said, but the actual words! This could only happen through the miracle of inspiration, and it was 'pictured' to Ezekiel as being given a book to eat. He took into himself the words God had written and when he had received them he was able to obey and 'speak with my words' (3:4). In all this Ezekiel remained a real person, called to make his own commitment and to obey God's word himself (2:8). The miracle of inspiration did not override or overrule his personality. As preacher of the word he had to be the first to obey it.

Day 2. Read Jeremiah 36:1–5, 17–18. A careful record

What a vivid picture! The Lord spoke (verses 2–3), Jeremiah dictated and Baruch wrote it all down (verses 4,18). The book was at one and the same time God's words, Jeremiah's words and Baruch's words. Each had his place. The Lord reveals what he wants to say; Jeremiah is inspired to receive and transmit it; and Baruch makes an exact record, word by word. This insight into the way one prophet safeguarded his message is true of the whole Bible: the word of God, the word of the human author, the word of the careful scribe.

Day 3. Read Isaiah 30:8–11. Focus on God

A 'tablet' (verse 8) is what we would call a 'hoarding'. The Chinese 'wall-newspaper' is, perhaps, a modern equivalent. This was how Isaiah made his message available to a wider public. But there is something else here too: we often think of the prophets as if they were primarily social reformers, challenging injustice and inequality. But actually, first and foremost, they spoke about God. This was what Isaiah's people found uncomfortable and unacceptable – 'stop confronting us with the Holy One' (verse 11).

Day 4. Read Amos 1:13 – 2:3. A world view: crimes against humanity

The prophets were social commentators too. Here we find Amos reviewing the crimes of the surrounding nations. (a) *Ammon the imperialist*, whose only concern was to 'extend his borders' and allowed no concern for human helplessness (the pregnant woman and the unborn child) to stand in the way (verse 13); (b) *Moab the vengeful*, who reached back into the past to exact retribution on a corpse (2:1)! The Ammonite wars are known in history; the act of Moab is known only in Amos. But all crimes against people are known in heaven and will unfailingly be judged and punished. A solemn and salutary thought for the savage world in which we live.

Day 5. Read Jeremiah 7:1–11. Religion without morality?

The Jerusalem Temple was the 'house' in which the Lord lived among his people. Because they had the temple they thought they had God too, and must therefore be safe whatever danger threatened. To Jeremiah a religion without moral commitment is a deception (verse 4). This is what he meant by the accusation that they were treating the house as robbers treat their den (verse 11) – a place of safety without thought of moral reformation! To Jeremiah (and all the prophets and all the Bible) a religion which failed to change lives was meaningless (James 1:26,27).

Day 6. Read Zechariah 2:1–5. Talking pictures

After the exile, Zechariah did what prophets often did: used pictures to tell the truth. In his time Jerusalem was still in ruins. There would have been much discussion about rebuilding plans and what the cost would be. The picture of stopping the surveyor from measuring the dimensions of old Jerusalem, was a vivid way of saying that the Lord is not limited to the past. With him we should always have larger, grander visions of what he will do in the future. This is a real message for us whether we think of our church or of our own lives: with God the best is always yet to be.

Day 7. Read Micah 4:1–5. The glorious future

What a marvellous prospect! – a world united round the Lord, magnetized by his truth, living at peace under his rule, without need either of weapons or of military training. This is what Jerusalem on its hill was always meant to be: a magnet to the world, holding the truth in order to share the truth (verse 2). While the New Testament stresses 'going out' to share the truth, it also agrees with the Old Testament that the Lord's people should be magnets: the quality of our individual and corporate lives 'attracting' those who are still outside. This is the point of Micah's determination to 'walk in the name of the Lord' (verse 5) – to live for him the life that speaks to others and draws them in.

Week 3: Amos, a typical prophet: disaster and hope

Day 1. Read Amos 2:4–12. The cardinal sin of the Lord's people

The formula 'three ... four' (2:1) is as if to say 'three sins would be enough, but the fourth – that's the last straw!' Up to the point of today's reading Amos has been addressing pagan nations (see Week 2, Day 4), but now he turns to the Lord's people in their two sections, Judah (verses 4,5) and Israel (verses 6–12), and finally both together (3:1–8). What does the Lord find to be the 'last straw' in the case of his people? To reject his 'law' ('teaching', verse 4) and to silence the voice of his prophets (verses 11,12). Of course, their social and religious misconduct matters (verses 6–8). What matters most of all, however, is that God taught them his truth and they would not learn; spoke to them by his prophets and they would not listen. To possess the word of God is to be judged by our use of this privilege.

Day 2. Read Amos 3:1–8. A word to be trusted

These verses focus on two things: (a) the unique relationship between the Lord and his people (verse 2); and (b) the significance of the voice of the prophet (verses 3–8). In this way Amos is continuing yesterday's teaching about the people of God possessing the word of God. Privilege brings peril (verses 1, 2): the more God entrusts to us, the more searching will be his enquiry into our response to our privileges; God's word cannot fail to be effective (verses 3–8).The seven pictures in verses 3–6 illustrate cause and effect. But there is a final cause which should bring about its proper effect: when the Lord speaks his word it is like the roar of a great lion and there should be a prompt response.

Day 3. Read Amos 4:4–13. Prepare to meet God

As Amos saw them people were extraordinarily religious and punctilious over it. Yet he saw all this as simply another way of sinning and of being self-pleasing (verses 4,5)! Meanwhile, through their circumstances – famine, drought, blight, plague and war, and calamity on a grand scale – the Lord was labouring to achieve what *he* wanted to see in them; a true repentance and return to God, a personal relationship in which sin was acknowledged and God sought (verses 6–11). If Jeremiah's people wanted religion without morality (Week 2, Day 5), Amos' people wanted religion without the personal dimension of repentance, reconciliation with God and a closeness of relationship with him – a (literally) 'coming right up to Me'.

Day 4. Read Amos 6:1–7. The penalty of complacency

In society around him Amos saw: unconcern regarding divine judgment (verse 3, the 'evil day'); oppressive rule (verse 3, 'terror'); self-indulgent life style (verse 4, 'beds, couches, choice lambs'); and lavish expenditure on luxury (verse 6, 'bowlful . . . lotions'). All this was bracketed about a complacent sense of their own security and a total unconcern about national welfare (verses 1–6). (Maybe 'Joseph' symbolizes those who could be hurt and dominated by more powerful interests, like Joseph in his brothers' power: heedlessness about the vulnerable members of society.) For such people Amos saw no hope.

Day 5. Read Amos 7:1–9. Hope and no hope

Two acts of divine judgment are prayed against (locusts and fire, verses 1–3,4–6) and, in allowing that prayer, the Lord is setting his face against any and every judgment which would totally destroy his people. But one judgment on them is neither prayed against nor averted – the plumbline (verses 7–9). The wall was (literally) 'built with a plumbline' and, when built, would be tested by the same plumbline. At the very beginning the Lord gave Moses a plumbline for building up the life of his people: the *law of God* as the standard for their conduct, and the *grace of God* (expressed in the atoning sacrifices) by which their lapses from obedience would be covered and forgiven. It was by this double standard they would be judged: did they commit themselves to obey? Did they run to God for forgiveness when they failed to obey (1 John 1:7.)?

Day 6. Read Amos 8:1–8. Market forces

What a vision of sweeping judgment (verses 3,8)! What could have caused such rage? (a) Exploitation in society (verse 4): the 'poor' and 'needy' are the financially disadvantaged, especially in the sense that their poverty made them easy game and readily exploitable. (b) An overriding interest in money-making (verse 5), and resentment if religion kept the shop closed! (c) Commercial dishonesty (verse 5), selling under weight and overcharging for it! (d) Using money and goods in bribery and corruption (verse 6). (e) Making a profit out of inferior goods (verse 6). All this, the Lord said, he will never forget (verse 7). This is the authentic voice of the prophet's social conscience.

Day 7. Read Amos 9:9–15. The sieve of the Lord

We saw (Day 5) how the Lord turned away from judgments that would destroy his people. Here is the glorious other side of the same divine purpose: he will sieve out his people (verse 9), removing every *complacent* sinner (verse 10 – those who deny all adverse consequence of their sin), and bring in the perfect kingdom of David, worldwide, with abundant prosperity, restoring his people to their proper possessions and security of tenure (verses 11–15).

Week 4: The greatest hope of all: the prophets and the coming Messiah

Day 1. Read Isaiah 9:1–7. The baby who is God and King
Isaiah lived through the dreadful Assyrian invasions (711–705 BC) and saw the northern areas fall to the conqueror (verse 1). Looking forward he also saw that where darkness first fell, light would first dawn (verse 2). A remarkable prediction in that Jesus spent his early life and his first ministry in Galilee. Isaiah saw the coming day as one of joy, victory and liberation (verses 3–4) – all because a baby was born, God himself come to birth, the bringer of peace, the inheritor of David's throne and the promised worldwide ruler (verses 6–7).

Day 2. Read Isaiah 25:1–9. Glad hope for all nations
The prophets, looking forward, saw all the world caught up into God's blessing. Isaiah 25 is in fact the song sung by the worldwide pilgrims as they throng home into the City of God. They come singing of deliverance (verses 1–5) and sit down to the Great Feast (verses 6–9) where every need is supplied, every shadow dispelled (including the shadow of death), every sorrow banished, and all that people ever expected from God fulfilled, the days of waiting amply rewarded.

Day 3. Read Ezekiel 34:22–31. The great Shepherd of the sheep
Kings were often depicted as shepherds, the carers of their people. When the David-to-be was foreseen, the model of the perfect Shepherd lay ready to hand. The picture corresponds to the past, present and future of the Christian –

the saving work of the Good Shepherd (John 10:14), the present care of the 'Shepherd and Overseer of your souls' (1 Peter 2:25), and the expectation of the coming Chief Shepherd (1 Peter 5:4).

Day 4. Read Isaiah 53:1–6. The servant Messiah: his birth and work

'The arm of the Lord' (verse 1) is shorthand for 'the Lord himself with his sleeves rolled up for action' (52:10; 51:9–10). Isaiah thus foresees God himself coming and growing up as a man among men (verses 2,3). In verse 5 'for' means 'because of'. Ours was the transgression, his the suffering, the purpose of which was to bring us peace with God. Trace in verse 6 what is true of *all*, what is true of *each* and what *the Lord* did about it. We can only marvel at the inspiration granted to Isaiah to foresee so minutely what would be fulfilled in the Lord Jesus.

Day 5. Read Isaiah 53:7–12. The servant Messiah: his death and life

Isaiah follows the course of the arrest (verse 7 – he could have resisted but chose not to), the injustice of the procedure, and his vicarious suffering (verse 8). The mysterious reference to (literally) 'the wicked men' and 'the rich man' in burial (verse 9), remained unexplained until it happened (Matthew 27:38,57). In all this the servant Messiah was guiltless (verse 9). Now comes the surprise! After all that bruising death, the Messiah is alive, 'prolonging his days' and active as the executor of the will of God (verse 10). Isaiah does not use the word 'resurrection' but he shows the Servant vigorously and actively alive after death and burial. Verse 12 sums up his greatness: (more accurately) 'Therefore I will give him the many as his portion and he will take the strong as his spoil.'

Day 6. Read Micah 5:1–5a. He is our peace

Here is another passage familiar in Christmas readings, and rightly so! David provided the model for much Old Testament expectation of the Messiah (see Days 1,3) – the best of the past foreshadowing the perfection of the future. Even David's town was to be the birthplace of the coming King. Yet the vision was not of a mere David 'lookalike'. The Old Testament does not give all the answers, but offers enigmas awaiting the fulfilled reality to explain them. So he will be born in Bethlehem, but his origins are 'from ancient times' (verse 2). Only the incarnation fits the picture and explains what Micah was grasping after. But he leaves unexplained how the coming ruler will himself be our Peace (verse 5). This has to await Ephesians 2:14–17.

Day 7. Read Isaiah 61:1–3. The transforming comforter

Isaiah completes his messianic preview (the King, Day 1; the Servant, Days 4,5) with the vision of the anointed One. This was the passage the Lord Jesus took as the 'text' of his first recorded sermon (Luke 4:16–19). Significantly he stopped reading at verse 2a, for his first coming was the year of favour and the 'day of vengeance' awaits his still-expected second coming (see 2 Thessalonians 1:7–9). The good news here (verse 1) is of his transforming power, touching and changing our sorrows, bondages and bereavements.

5

The Voice of Wisdom

Proverbs: the wise life

There is more sheer fun in reading the book of Proverbs than in any other portion of Scripture. Its observations of life are so sharp and its illustrations so apt! Were interfering busybodies ever put in their place with such absurd accuracy as 26:17? How well 27:14 identifies with one who is not 'an early morning person'! And the sorely tried spirit which lies behind 17:12 will find an echo with everyone whose acquaintances include a talkative bore.

But the same sharpness and accuracy looks over the whole of life in this deeply practical book. It is very frank about the frightful 'own goal' scored by the sexually promiscuous (2:18; 5:3–6; 7:24–27) and even sees an adulterous relationship itself – however entrancing it may at that moment seem to the participants – as a visitation of divine wrath (22:14). By contrast it affirms the delights of true marriage in a refreshingly plain-spoken way (5:18–19). But it is too observant of life to see marriage as a cure-all: things can be sadly otherwise and 19:13; 21:9,19; 25:24; and 27:15 reflect how, for an ill-matched couple, the bad can rapidly become the unbearable!

We would explore Proverbs almost endlessly. Very often it just glides over the surface of life without comment, saying and showing 'how things are' – the exasperations caused by the unreliable (10:26; 25:19; 26:6); the influence that money (19:4) and a well-placed gift (21:14) can exercise; the harm done by sly innuendo (16:30), even though such a person will not for ever get away with it (6:12–15); the destructive tongue (11:9; 18:21; 25:23) and the healing tongue (15:1; 16:24; 25:11). At other times it probes deeper – the accurate psychology of 4:23; the exposure of the too-ready solution and the 'quick fix' (18:13; 29:20); the sound work ethic which it commends both positively and negatively (10:4,5; 24:30–34). But, as we shall now see, there is more to Proverbs than a jumble of observations (however sharp) and precepts (however sound).

The Lord: Wise Creator, righteous world ruler

We take the temperature of the book of Proverbs more accurately by comparing two sayings which lie very close to each other in the book:

> Do not move an ancient boundary stone
>   set up by your forefathers (22:28).

In an agricultural economy, land tenure is the basis of social stability. Boundaries reflect a situation received from a respected past, to be cherished and perpetuated.

In 23:10, the same thought occurs, with a significant addition:

> Do not move an ancient boundary stone
>   or encroach on the fields of the fatherless,
> for their Defender is strong;
>   he will take up their case against you.

The next-of-kin

'Defender' translates a word used for the 'next-of-kin', the one who has the right to intervene, taking all the needs and troubles of his helpless relative upon himself as though they were his own. This lovely Old Testament custom is illustrated in the story of Ruth and Boaz (*cf.* Ruth 3:12–13; 4:3–10), and the word itself is frequently used of the Lord as the 'Kinsman-Redeemer' of his people, the one who takes on himself the debts of his people and pays the price for them (Psalm 19:14; 78:35; Isaiah 49:26; 63:16).

So we see that there is more to the 'landmark' saying than first met the eye. The Lord is involved in it, observes when it is breached, identifies with the offended party and takes action against the offender. This theological basis of the good life runs right through Proverbs. Its individual precepts may seem as haphazard and unrelated as the stones that litter Dartmoor but, like those stones, they are aspects of an underlying bed of solid granite, the wise Creator and righteous world-ruler.

The Lord's wisdom

Following the Dartmoor analogy, just as there the bedrock makes its presence felt by thrusting upwards in small outcrops and great formations, so the underlying theology of Proverbs breaks surface in nearly one hundred verses which refer to 'God' or 'the Lord'.

We learn that wisdom is the Lord's possession. We need not discuss whether 8:12–31 (especially verses 22–31) understood wisdom as a divine person or whether, for vividness, it personified the idea of wisdom. Either way, of course, the passage prepares for the New Testament revelation of the Lord Jesus (1 Corinthians 1:24,30; Colossians 2:3), but its basic claim is clear that even before any creative work was undertaken, wisdom resided with the Lord and was uniquely his, an attribute (to say the least) of God in eternity. The same link between the Lord and wisdom is found in 1:29 where to *hate knowledge* is the same as *not to choose to fear the Lord*.

Wisdom in creation

The creation itself displays the wisdom of the Lord. This is beautifully worked out in 8:27–31 where wisdom accompanied the Lord in the creation, in ordering heaven and earth, and itself/himself rejoiced in the finished product (verse 31). There is also the direct statement of 3:19,20.

By wisdom the Lord laid the earth's foundations,
    by understanding he set the heavens in place;
  by his knowledge the deeps were divided,
    and the clouds let drop the dew.

But in Proverbs, as in the rest of the Old Testament, the Creator has a more far-reaching relation with the creation than simply as the One who originated heaven and earth. He is also the wise director of world affairs (21:1); it is he who decides the course of individual life (16:1,9); and even in small details that would appear to happen by chance, it is still the Lord who settles the issue (16:33).

The wise and the good
It is this wise Creator who reveals the distinction between good and evil and decides what is the good life. It is his glory to keep things to himself should he so decide (25:2). Consequently wisdom can only be ours if and when he gives it, and knowledge if and when he speaks it (2:6). But he has indeed spoken so that Proverbs is able to say what it is that he hates (6:16–19), and to contrast what he abhors with what he delights in (11:1,20; 12:22; 15:8; *etc.*).

Two avenues of life open out before us and the issues are plain. The Lord observes all life and every thought and action (15:3,11; 16:2; 20:27), not passively, however, but as One active in life in terms of rewards and punishments. He feeds the righteous and thwarts the wicked (10:3); he is a fortress to run to in trouble (10:29; 18:10); he destroys the proud, stands by the helpless (15:25), is far from the wicked but hears the prayer of the righteous (15:29). He is purposefully active in everything (16:4), morally alert to avenge (20:22) but also to withhold vengeance where to inflict it would prompt sinful reactions in the one who has been wronged (24:17).

Wisdom and true human life
It follows from all this, and from the many more references which could be offered under each heading, that the life which conforms to God's wisdom, and to his standards of right and wrong, is the proper life for everyone on earth, the truly human life. There are three reasons for this. First, it matches the constitution of the world in which we live (3:19–20). Secondly, there is a joyful 'match' between wisdom itself/himself and mankind

as created and intended by the Creator (8:31), so that, in living out the life of wisdom we are 'fulfilling' ourselves, being what we were meant to be. Thirdly, the life of wisdom is under the active blessing of the Lord, as the verses quoted above show.

The purpose of the book of Proverbs

Why, then, is the book of Proverbs in the Bible? Just for this purpose – to reveal, teach and direct us to this life of fulfilment and blessing. Its precepts, whether encouraging or warning, are meant to lead us into the life that matches both our own true nature and the perfect will of God.

See how this is put in Proverbs 1:2–7.

Verse 2. By this book we 'attain', (literally) 'know', what *wisdom* is and we are launched into God's educative programme (*discipline*); we acquire *understanding, i.e.* the ability to see to the heart of things.

Verse 3. This educative programme (*disciplined*) brings prudence, that is, true good sense in the management of life; we learn to do *what is right* (before God), *just* (making right decisions) and *fair* or straightforward.

Verse 4. In ourselves we are *simple*, lacking and needing guiding principles of life, open to impulse and influence. But this book can give *prudence*, shrewd perceptiveness, replacing our natural ignorance with *knowledge*, rescuing us from floundering through life by giving *discretion*, a sense of purpose.

Verse 5. Even those who are already to any degree *wise* need its help to gain fuller *learning*, a 'grasp' of the truth; and those who are already *discerning* can receive fuller *guidance*, skill in formulating plans and plotting life's course.

Verse 6. In this way things that were formerly enigmas and conundrums yield up their secrets.

Verse 7. In all this the primary factor is *the fear of the Lord*, for wisdom cannot be separated from the Lord as its source. Wisdom is, in fact, the Lord revealing himself as a way of life for his people to practise. Because this is so, 1:29

identifies the wise life with the fear of the Lord; 2:5 shows the other side of the same coin – that pursuing wisdom leads to fearing the Lord; according to 3:7; 8:13; 16:6, fearing the Lord finds its counterpart in shunning evil; and 10:27; 14:26–27; 19:23; 22:4; 23:17–18 motivate us to fear the Lord by the blessings that will follow. But, of course, this is not abject fear. It is the reverential fear spoken of in 1 Peter 1:17–19, the sensitive dread of hurting the One who loves us so.

Job: life is not all that simple!

Proverbs is full of crisp commands, black-and-white situations and seemingly automatic promises. It would be easy to overlook that it also contains passages like 3:9–12. Here is an apparently foolproof recipe for prosperity! But before we have time to launch ourselves into it, we find that there is another side to life: a darker side of discipline and rebuke.

Proverbs recognizes this but does not wrestle with it: that is the province reserved for the book of Job.

Unexplained suffering
Headlong, Job drops us into life's greatest enigma, personal suffering that is never explained. And to the end, it was never explained to Job why he was despoiled of his property, bereaved of his children (1:13–19), deprived of his health and alienated from his wife (2:7–9); Job's friends (2:11–13) came to sympathize and stayed to explain (4:1 – 25:6), but their explanations were doomed to failure because they depended on an estimate of Job (*e.g.* 18:5–21) which contradicted the Job that God knew (1:8; 2:3) and the life that Job had lived (31:1–40).

Even we who from the start are let into the secret that Job's travail is a deliberately set up contest between the Lord and Satan, are never allowed to know why the Lord initiated it to begin with (1:8). It is all one great puzzle, and the fact of the matter is that life is like that. More often than not suffering is the essence of the problem of making sense out of life, but it is far from being the only problem.

110

The problematic Lord: all-wise, all-just, all-powerful

If there was no God there would be no problem. For example, if we believed that everything happens by chance we would face suffering and say the equivalent of 'That's the way the cookie crumbles'. Or again, if we believed that the world is run by human decision and freewill we would face suffering and say, 'It stands to reason that we make a mess of the job.'

It is only when we bring God into the equation that suffering is felt to be a problem, and the Lord's speeches from 38:1 onwards in the book of Job tell us why this is so.

38:2 – 39:30. A series of baffling questions touching on the wonders of the created world (38:4–38) and of the animal kingdom (38:39 – 39:30), designed to show the *wisdom* of God which baffles the human mind.

40:1,6–14. Job who has questioned God's justice (verses 2,8) is ironically invited to undertake the moral government of the world (verses 9–14). Of course he cannot, for only God can exercise this *perfect justice*.

40:15–24; 41:1–34. Two horrendous creatures are introduced: Behemoth, 'the Beast of Beasts', and the awesome mythical Leviathan. These cannot be mastered by mankind (40:24; 41:8) but are subject to their Creator (40:19). See, then, how great is the *power* of God (41:10–11)!

Think about it! This is the God of the Bible, all-wise, all-just, all-powerful! If only we could deny any one of these three attributes of God, the world we live in would become totally logical, without a problem in sight.

Suppose he were wise and just but lacking in power, or wise and powerful but lacking justice, or just and powerful but lacking wisdom! Each supposition provides a bracket into which to put every problematic experience of life, for it would simply be one of those occasions on which his justice or wisdom or power was not up to the job! We would have the perfect explanation! 'Of course,' we would say, 'he is all-wise and all-just but unfortunately – as now – he does not always have the power to do what he wants. Or 'unfortunately he is not always wise', or 'not always just'. All life would be logical again!

But if he is indeed the almighty God, and every experience in life must ultimately be 'down' to him, and if everything is at one and the same time an exact expression of what is right and wise, then we can only join Job in coming to rest in humility and trust on this truly sovereign God in his infallible wisdom, unswerving righteousness and absolute power (40:3–5; 42:1–6).

Faith and resolute devotion

This call to faith is the major lesson of the book of Job. The truth is expressed equally beautifully, but more briefly, in Psalm 23:2–4. Sometimes life is green pastures and quiet waters (verse 2); sometimes it is the valley of the shadow of death (verse 4). The connecting link between these variations is *paths of righteousness* (verse 3), paths that are right in the Shepherd's sight, that make sense to him. To the sheep, life is a baffling kaleidoscope of fluctuating fortunes, but the Shepherd knows. It is he who decides, directs, and accompanies. And the sheep can rest content.

This is the point Job reached at the end, but it is not the point at which the book began. The whole drama started the moment when the Lord's delighted commendation of his servant (1:8) was countered by Satan's scornful yet penetrating question: Does Job fear God for nothing? (1:9). That's it! Will Job still be the Lord's man when every advantage arising from faith in God has been removed and seems to be contradicted?

Would we? Would we celebrate Christmas, marooned alone on a desert island, with goods and family all lost at sea?

The life of wisdom, says Proverbs, can be described, offered as a code and a life style to be followed. Indeed so, says Job, but it is also a life of faith – the faith that trusts in the all-wise, all-sovereign, all-just Lord; the faith that goes all the way in devoted perseverance with him.

Ecclesiastes: a world that refuses to make sense

The third great 'wisdom' book in the Bible is Ecclesiastes, and what a problem it presents as soon as we open its pages! What a dark view of life! What gloomy pessimism!

Here is someone who undertook to see all life through the spectrum of wisdom (1:13), and no ordinary wisdom at that! (1:16). He gave himself to a full experience of life – pleasure and fun (2:1–2) – but without losing his grip on wisdom (2:3); he went into property development and estate management (2:4), a retinue of servants to attend him (2:7), money-making (2:8) – but retaining wisdom throughout (2:9). And what was his conclusion? 'Everything ['The whole lot'] was meaningless, a chasing after the wind; nothing was gained under the sun' (2:11). Oh dear!

Another ingredient in life

The sort of material sketched above from chapters 1 and 2 of Ecclesiastes could be followed right through the book.

Work is meaningless (2:17); people die like beasts (3:18); mourners go uncomforted (4:1); would it be better not to have lived at all (4:2–3)? Virtue goes unrewarded, even forgotten (4:13–16); wealth does not necessarily bring enjoyment (6:1–2). In fact, life is just dreadfully and irretrievably cussed (7:13).

But alongside all this there is another set of truths: when God comes into life, satisfaction and fulfilment come with him (2:24,25); in fact, for all its variables, its changes and chances, life is apportioned out by him (3:1–8) and everything, somehow, has its own beauty (3:11); the difficulties of life are divine testings (3:18); for all that life is hard, there is a life with God to be cultivated (5:1); indeed life itself, received as a gift of God, is good and proper ('a good which is lovely', 5:18). It is true that we have no control over the future and must await its onset no matter what it brings, and nothing can shield us from its barbs (9:1–2). Yet life itself is a joy (9:9–10), a favour from God; the one thing certain about the future is divine judgment (11:9;

12:14), but God has revealed his way and will to us, so that we may live to please him (12:11–13).

Life's like that!

What a muddle the whole book of Ecclestiastes seems! One minute we are deep in pessimism and the game is not worth the candle; another minute life is delightful and fulfilling. One minute we wander and grope in the dark; another minute we have clear directions about living with God and pursuing the good life. One minute we do not know what happens after death – people die as inconsequentially as flies; another minute, there is an eternal future and a way of being prepared for it.

But it has to be like that, because life is like that – not the life of the unbeliever, but of the believer – our life is like that!

Some have suggested that Ecclesiastes is an attempt to see what life would look like without God, the inevitable pessimisms, disappointments and dark ignorances of man without divine revelation. But, no, that is not the point of Ecclesiastes.

Its constant cry is that life is (as the NIV puts it) 'meaningless' (*e.g.* 1:2; 12:8). The word is not easy to translate by any single English equivalent, but as it is used in Ecclesiastes it means this, that 'life does not add up'. The ceaseless round of human history (1:4) and of 'nature' (1:5–7) does not seem to be going anywhere: what does it all add up to? People give themselves to pleasure, property, luxury: what does it all add up to? No sooner is life gladdened by a birth, than it is saddened by a death; suffering comes without warning, out of a clear blue sky; there is oppression but not comfort, virtue but not reward; work but not fulfilment.

Can the believer explain these things any more than the unbeliever? Faced with the biting and blighting sufferings of life, its sicknesses and deaths, its disabled and disappointed people, great ones and loved ones alike flying forgotten as a dream: what does it all add up to? Can we, any more than the unbeliever, answer the agonized and despairing cry of a tragic race, 'Why, Why, Why?'

Job faced the single problem of suffering; Ecclesiastes is a wider-ranging book. It raises the problem of life itself, and, like Job, has no explanation of life's problems. It cannot reduce life to a single logical system in which all problems are solved, but it does have a recipe for living!

Think of it this way: facing life is like standing looking at a great wall, extending endlessly in each direction, blocking off the future. On this wall are written all the problems and groanings of life, and all its lightness and joys as well. These are the things that await us, lying inescapably across our path. But when we get close to the wall we see that there is a door. It is labelled, 'God, revelation, faith': it is an invitation to enter the future under God, in the light of truth and along the way of trust.

So we enter. We are now in the arena of faith, but we discover at once that the way of faith is an about-turn. We are now walking in the opposite direction to the road we were on before we became believers. The wall is still there, still blocking off the future, still inscribed with all the groanings, problems and potential happiness of life, and we must still face them and we still cannot explain them. Now, however, we are coming to them, living among them, bearing their burden, rejoicing in their joys on a different footing, with God rather than without him, living the life of faith in a world that does not add up.

That is precisely 'where we are' and Ecclesiastes is a tract for our times!

**A Scenic Route Through
Old Testament Wisdom**

**Listen to the voice of wisdom discussing life and
directing conduct**

Four weeks of short daily Bible readings with brief notes

Week 1: Proverbs – the way of wisdom

Day 1. Read Proverbs 1:8–19. Decisiveness

In the Bible truth is not truly known until it changes the
way we live. Instruction and teaching lead to outward
beauty of life (verses 8–9). But such a life never goes
unchallenged, and Proverbs now describes a young person
facing a typical temptation to veer from the wise path
(verses 10–19) – to exploit other people for the sake of
self-gain and to 'keep in with your mates'. But such a life
offends God; it is sin: and sin always boomerangs (verses
18–19). Characteristically, Proverbs begins by calling us to
side decisively with the way of wisdom.

Day 2. Read Proverbs 1:20–33. Urgency

The message of this section is simple: the voice of wisdom
is readily available, but if it is ignored the day will come
when our cry for wisdom will be ignored and we will get
what we have chosen. Life is like that, so we should give
close attention to the voice of God teaching us in the word
of God. This saves us from living without guiding principles, from cynical mockery of true values, and from
becoming moral fatheads.

Day 3. Read Proverbs 2:1–11. Getting down to it

Notice the balance between *Then* and *For* in verses 5–6 and
9–10. When we work hard at wisdom *then* understanding
comes (verse 5), *for* it is in this way that the Lord gives
wisdom (6–8). When he gives wisdom, *then* (verse 9) we
understand how to live, *for* wisdom grips our hearts and

becomes a protective force in our lives (verses 10–11). The conditions on which we may enjoy these benefits are open-minded acceptance of the word of God and memorization (verse 1), attentiveness and mental application (verse 2), prayer (verse 3), and committed searching for the truth in its intrinsic value (verse 4).

Day 4. Read Proverbs 3:1–13. The Lord first
Life is a mix of good times and bad, prosperity and adversity. Over it all is the Lord, who makes things plain (verse 6) and prosperous (verses 9–10) and who also disciplines and rebukes (verses 11–12). Since all life is thus straight from the Lord's hand, our primary concern is not health and fitness programmes (verse 8) or market forces (verse 10), but trusting (verse 5) and honouring him (verse 9), and bowing to his will with glad submissiveness (verses 11–12).

Day 5. Read Proverbs 5:1–20. Personal purity
When you read right through Proverbs you will find that today's theme of sexual purity and married joy is recurrent, and basic to the wise life. Proverbs hides nothing: sexual misbehaviour, for all its promised sweetness, brings death (verses 3–5), broken health (verse 11), belated self-awareness and public disgrace (verses 12–14). How fulfilling and entrancing by contrast is God's plan of marriage (verses 15–19)! And not only in sex but over the whole arena of life. The *why?* of verse 20 challenges us to recognize that holiness wins every time over sin.

Day 6. Read Proverbs 8:12–31. Wisdom in person
Whether we understand that wisdom is revealed here as a distinct divine person within the Godhead, or that it is a dramatic personification of a divine attribute, the passage prepares us for the revelation of the Lord Jesus as the wisdom of God (1 Corinthians 1:24,30; 2:6–7; Colossians 2:3). As we read we can turn every thought into worship and praise of him in whom true wisdom is seen (verses 12–14), who is King of kings (verses 15–16) in whom we find wisdom and its rewards (verses 17–21); the eternal

One (verses 22–26), present in the work of creation (verses 27–31) and delighting in the divine handiwork.

Day 7. Read Proverbs 9:1–18. Decisions, decisions!
The first nine chapters of Proverbs are a unity in a way that is not true of the rest of the book. Note, therefore, how we return today to the thoughts of the first two days above: in this life alternative voices call to us (verses 1,13). The one has food in abundance, and hers to give (verses 4–5); the other invites to a stolen banquet (verse 17). The one calls to life (verse 6); the other opens the door to death (verse 18). In one case, lack of guiding principle (*simple*, verse 6) is transformed into wisdom and learning (verse 9); in the other, those who lack guiding principles (verse 16) are conducted to their death (verse 18). The choice is ours.

Week 2: Proverbs – directives for the wise

Day 1. Read Proverbs 10:22–32. Types and talk
The fool (verse 23) is not so much the person who does not stop to think, as the one who has not got the clues or the abilities to think straight, the fathead. By contrast the wise learn from the wisdom of God. It is not accidental that Proverbs moves directly to the contrast between the righteous and the wicked (verses 24,28,29,30,32). One thing leads to another! Typically in Proverbs people are known by the way they talk (31–32). Sins of speech are in Proverbs' top three.

Day 2. Read Proverbs 12:28 – 13:9. Righteousness
Righteousness gives, guards, and promotes life (verses 12:28; 13:6,9), wickedness brings overthrow and death verses 6,9). This is the main thrust of this group of sayings and constitutes a call to moral commitment (verse 5). But the sayings about listening and talking (verses 1–3) need to be pondered, as do the sharp observations that life must not be judged by appearance (verse 7), and no

one bothers to kidnap a poor man (verse 8)! It is this 'mix' of deep instruction, warning and street-wise comment that makes Proverbs so rich.

Day 3. Read Proverbs 15:33 – 16:7. Living for the Lord

A passage unique in Proverbs in that eight verses in turn mention the Lord. He is the sovereign who has the last word in all our plans (16:1) and governs everything for his own purposes (16:4); the fear of the Lord (the loving, careful reverence of 1 Peter 1:17) directs (15:33) and restrains (16:6); he knows and appraises our hearts (16:2,5); he is active for those who live so as to please him (16:7); and the truly successful life comes when we commit ('roll on to the Lord' – like a burden we are glad to be rid of) all our work and all our plans (16:3).

Day 4. Read Proverbs 23:12–19. Putting your heart into it

In these sayings the heart is given characteristic prominence. It matters what things preoccupy our hearts (verse 12), and also the ambitions and aspirations we cherish there (verse 19), the desires to which we give heart-room. The heart is ours to control, shutting out envy (literally 'covet'), insisting rather that it should be zealous for (better 'covet') reverence (verse 17). The heart settled in his wisdom delights our Father (verse 15). The heart is, of course, the whole person from the inner point of view: thought, desire, imagination, conscience, ambition. What we think, we are, says Proverbs.

Day 5. Read Proverbs 26:12–27. It takes all sorts!

What a collection of very believable people! The conceited person – why there's more hope for a fathead (verse 12)! The idler/wastrel/work-shy for whom any excuse will do (verse 13), bed is always the preferred option (verse 14), any effort is too exhausting (verse 15) – but from his armchair vantage, how very judicious (verse 16)! Meet the busybody (verse 17); the inveterate 'life and soul of the party' (verses 18–19); the tragic consequences of tittle-tattle and argumentativeness (verses 20–22); the hard gloss of earnestness and charm hiding evil and malice (verses 23–26). But there is a justice that works its way out (verses 26–27).

Day 6. Read Proverbs 27:18–27. In praise of diligence

Just as Proverbs has it in for the indolent, it loves the diligent and commends the diligent life (look back to Week 1, Day 3). Verse 18 is a typical mixture of sound advice and wordly wisdom – the way of prosperity and the way of promotion. But underneath it is the sound principle of living in God's world, not in man's. This is why the flocks (verse 23), the new growth (verse 25), lambs and goats (verse 26) and milk (verse 27) are stressed. For your investments may let you down (verse 24), but your ground will not. Underneath its hard-headed approach, Proverbs is resting on divine promises (Genesis 8:22).

Day 7. Read Proverbs 30:1–9. Ignorance and knowledge

The names given here are all unknown, but from what he said Agur was well qualified to be reckoned among the wise. First, he was content to live within the revelation God had given. There was much he did not know, and could not until One came from heaven (John 3:12–13), but he knew that God had spoken, a pure and complete word, enabling us to trust and find refuge in him (verses 5–6). Secondly, he was content to commit the circumstances of his life to God, concerned only to maintain loyalty and to live according to what the Lord had revealed ('the name') of himself (verses 7–9).

Week 3: You have heard of the patience of Job (James 5:11)

Day 1. Read Job 1:1–22. God's man and God's mystery

Job comes before us as a man to whom God bore witness as blameless and upright (verse 8). This at once rules out the possibility that the suffering to come was provoked by sin. But what was its cause? We are never told! The Lord calls Satan's attention to Job (verse 8, *cf*. 2:3) and sets the limits of his liberty of action against Job (verse 12, *cf*. 2:6), but keeps to himself his reasons for doing so. The Lord does what pleases him in heaven and earth (Psalm 135:6; *cf*. 1 Samuel 3:18) and that's the end of it! But Satan is as much subject to his sovereignty as is Job. What a position of responsibility Job has, for unrevealed heavenly purposes depend on how he acts and reacts under stress.

Day 2. Read Job 3:11–26. Why, why, why?

Job's friends have come to comfort him (2:11–13) and with them he shares the blackness of his perplexity in five 'why's' (verses 11,12,16,20,23). If life is like this, why was he allowed to survive birth – indeed, why was he born at all? What is the point of life if it means only an unfulfilled longing for death? Why does God give life only to build impenetrable hedges around it? Questions are not in themselves wrong; they are part of our humanity, for God created us to want and need explanations. But questions more often deny God than affirm him, as Job did in verse 23. Even when it is at its most unacceptable and inexplicable, it is still the life God has apportioned to us.

Day 3. Read Job 9:1–13. Let God be God!

By this point two of Job's friends have spoken and one is yet to speak. From different angles they have one explanation: sin in Job's life has brought him calamity. Job knows this is not true (and so do we), but one thing he knows for certain: God is God. He cannot be understood (verses 1–11), nor can he be called to account (verses 12–13). Oddly, but for a reason we shall presently discover, this truth gives Job no rest. Yet it is the surest resting-place of all in trouble. In his majestic wisdom and power the Sovereign of all creation knows what he is doing (verses 4–10)! Don't call him to account for his ways; accept and rest.

Day 4. Read Job 19:13–27. Suffering and certainty

Job saw the hand of God now in all things (verse 21) – the hand from which we can never be plucked (John 10:27–29). He also foresaw the fellowship of God then (verses 25–26) when all the testing is past. He is here with me now; I will be there with him then. *Redeemer* (verse 25), the next-of-kin who takes all the trials, troubles, needs, inadequacies of his helpless relative as if they were his own and deals with them, himself paying every debt.

Day 5. Read Job 28:12–28. Knowing is no comfort

If you have time, read this whole marvellous poem. Man can search out almost everything (verses 3,9), but is there a mine for wisdom (verse 12)? Man is at a loss (verse 13); so is all creation (verse 14); money cannot buy it (verses 15–19); searching upward or downward reveals nothing (verses 21–22). God alone knows (verses 23–27, see Week 1, Day 6), and we only know what he chooses to reveal (verse 28). But verse 28 is exactly how Job had lived (1:8) – and look where it brought him! Divine revelation is the only basis for life, but it brings no guarantee of ease or immunity.

Day 6. Read Job 38:31–35; 40:8–14; 41:15–19. God: wisdom, justice, power

Chapters 38 – 39 drive home the measureless wisdom of God, exemplified in Creation. In 40:8–14 the Lord (sarcastically) invites Job to undertake the moral government of the world, implying that only God can rule with perfect justice. 40:15 – 41:34 describe two terrifying powerful monsters (40:15; 41:1), quite beyond man's power to master but subject to God. Job already knew all this about God – that he is endless in wisdom, absolute in justice and sovereign in power – but not till the Lord himself came and said it to him (38:1) did the truth become his comfort, for he found himself in personal communion with an infinite God in whom he could rest. We have the voice of God in the word of God.

Day 7. Read Job 42:1–16. Home at last

The end of the story is not just a 'happy ever after' senti-
mentality. The Lord proposed a fearful, but limited test
(chapters 1,2); now that Job has passed the test, justice
requires restoration. And after the manner of the Lord's
gracious dealings, not just restoration but double! Even in
the matter of children he has double – though the first
family is gone to God. Well could James refer not only to
Job's patience but also to the Lord's ultimate outcome
(James 5:11) – full of compassion indeed. See 2 Corinthians 4:16 – 5:1; Revelation 7:9–17.

Week 4: Living in a world that does not add up

Day 1. Read Ecclesiastes 1:2–11. Nothing is going anywhere!

A hymn addresses God as 'Eternal Ruler of the ceaseless
round', and that is exactly what Ecclesiastes sees: human
life (verse 4), day and night (verse 5), climatic changes
(verse 6), the constant cycling of water (verse 7) – and no
matter how enquiry is pursued (verse 8) it all seems to add
up to nothing (verse 9). As a general truth, nothing really
novel appears (verse 10)! Even the most dramatic scientific
discoveries are only the uncovering of what has always
been so! So what does it all mean – if anything? The eye
looks out on 'meaninglessness' – 'vanity' said the older
translations – that does not 'add up'.

Day 2. Read Ecclesiastes 2:24 – 3:22. But God is in business!

Even though, to our eye, life does not 'add up' there is
satisfaction in it (2:24–25). There is a life of God-pleasing,
bringing blessing and, what's more, it is all going somewhere: to the final settlement when the meek shall inherit
the earth (2:26). The experiences which do not 'add up' for
me, make sense to God who apportions all the contrasting
experiences of life (3:1–8), adding beauty to everything in
its time (3:10). He wills our joy in the present (3:12), moves

to judgment in the future (3:15), apportioning tests to bring us to a true self-awareness, lest we live purely animal lives (3:18).

Day 3. Read Ecclesiastes 5:10–20. Market forces and spiritual bequests

Typical of its sharp perceptiveness of life, Ecclesiastes turns its microscope on money, seen by people and governments alike as the panacea – but is it? After all, experience shows that it does not in fact bring satisfaction (verses 10–12); that it is highly vulnerable to change and chance (verses 13–14); and that death cancels all bank balances (verses 15–17). It is very different when life, joy in life, and heart-satisfaction are all seen as God's gift (verses 18–20).

Day 4. Read Ecclesiastes 8:2 – 9:1. Living with an unknown future

How oddly life works out (fails to 'add up') in respect of virtue and reward, crime and punishment! A person tries to live prudently within the given framework of society but misery still weighs heavily (verses 2–6). The only certain future is death (verses 7–8)! People hurtfully dominate each other (verse 9). The wicked cynically practise religion and society praises them, and this leads to social deterioration (verses 10–11). Faith takes a different view of things (verses 12–13), but the problem remains: moral rewards are reversed (verse 14). No-one can make sense of life (verses 16–17). So what is there to do? Rest in God's hands (9:1).

Day 5. Read Ecclesiastes 9:17 – 10:7. The thinking life

9:13–16 asserts that wisdom is better than folly. The present verses comment on that. Two different words are translated 'fool/folly': in 9:17 and 10:2 the 'fool' is the 'fathead' who lives without thinking; in 10:1,3,6 he is the 'thickhead' who cannot think straight even when he tries. The way of wisdom is not easy – it meets with loud and effective opposition (9:17,18); it can easily be spoiled

(10:1), but it characterizes the properly constituted person (10:2), faces life calmly (10:4), but by no means always or automatically succeeds (10:5–7). Uncomfortable – but realistic and all too true!

Day 6. Read Ecclesiastes 10:12–20. Words and work

9:7–10 advocated gusto in enjoying life. The present verses explore this, first in the realm of speech. Gusto in talk is the sign of a fool (verses 12–15) who, when all comes to all, could not even tell you how to get to the town centre! Besides, even the unspoken thought can get you into dire trouble (verse 20). Secondly, in the realm of diligence: in government, the good things of life must be subordinate to the needs of the duties of life (verses 16–17); privately, where there is idleness there is no income to repair the roof (verse 18); enjoyment is all very well, but there must be a sound income to undergird needs (verse 19). All this, too, is realistic thinking.

Day 7. Read Ecclesiastes 11:9 – 12:14. Conclusions

Oh yes, life is for living (9:7–10), and not least when you are young (11:9). But there are other considerations too: judgment is coming (11:9); and death is coming (12:1–7). Life is like day, always darkening towards night, like changeable weather, always coming on to rain (12:2); like a great house falling into decay – its upkeep exceeds the strength of the residents (12:3). Morning tasks (grinding) are all that can be managed, so bolt the doors (12:4). Sleep is broken by a sound as light as bird song – even though hearing is not what it used to be. All sorts of things seem threats and there is no longer a spring in the step; yes, death is on its way (12:5–8). Life does not add up – unless ... unless there are words of truth (12:9–10), to stimulate (*goads*), to give security (*nails*, 12:11), words from the Shepherd, God himself. This is the real conclusion – to reverence and obey (12:13).

6

The Voice of God

Instead of Columbus 'discovering America', suppose the American Indians had journeyed east to tell us about themselves and about the marvellous land to the west where they lived. The Old Testament is like that: it is not the account of a human voyage of discovery, searching for God, but of God coming to tell us about himself.

Of course, now that we have the Old Testament (and the rest of the Bible) we can go on a voyage of discovery ourselves to find out more about what God has revealed and (always, as the main purpose of the book) to know God and Jesus Christ whom he sent (John 17:3), to 'grow in the grace and knowledge of our Lord and Saviour Jesus Christ' (2 Peter 3:18).

Progressive revelation

The Old Testament is the beginning of God's progressive revelation of himself.

Truth and more truth
Hebrews 1:1 notes that God revealed himself 'at many times and in various ways' in the past. Adam received a bit of God's truth, and so did Noah; God spoke more fully to Abraham, unveiling more of himself and his purposes. He revealed himself supremely in the Old Testament through Moses. Progressive revelation is a movement from truth to more truth and so to full truth.

Some things were for their own time only, later to be set aside. This happened, for example, in the case of the restrictive food laws (*e.g.* Deuteronomy 14:1–21) which

127

were repealed by the Lord Jesus (Mark 7:19); the same happened, too, with many of the laws designed to regulate the life of the people of God when, in the Old Testament, they were a political state with their own government. A radical change took place when the earthly kingdom of the Lord's people was replaced by the kingdom of the Lord Jesus Christ under him as King (John 18:36).

Yet, even when laws are openly or implicitly set aside, they still have a testimony to bear to the truth. Take the food laws as an example. They were part of the way the Lord insisted that his people live a distinct life, separate from other peoples on earth. This is still a divine requirement (2 Corinthians 6:14 – 7:1), and still applicable to the realm of appetite and indulgence. In the same way, though we are no longer constituted as an earthly kingdom, we are still concerned for equity, for the integrity of the courts, for exactness and effectiveness of criminal law, for social righteousness, and all the other things the old laws were designed to express and safeguard in the kingdom of the first David.

The inadequate and the complete

As we follow the course of progressive revelation we also see the inadequate becoming the complete.

Throughout Old Testament times the Lord dealt with his people through animal sacrifice, and attached real and precious promises to the shedding of animal blood. For example, he promised atonement (Leviticus 1:4) and forgiveness (Leviticus 4:20). These were not deceitful promises for, as we saw in the Psalms, the people of the Old Covenant church actually lived in the good of peace with God, rejoicing in him in worship, knowing him as the God of mercy, forgiveness and redemption.

The Old Testament nowhere said to its people that the animal sacrifices they made were a temporary expedient, or that the benefits they enjoyed through the animal sacrifices depended on a perfect sacrifice yet to be made in the far future, or anything like that. The Lord made promises and he attached his promises to the shedding of blood. His people believed his promises and he kept them.

Yet within the Old Testament people began to realize, from time to time, that something better was needed. David was perplexed that his sins of murder and adultery were not covered by sacrificial provision (Psalm 51:16), yet discerned in the Lord a covering mercy that went beyond what the sacrifices could promise (Psalm 51:7–9).

Isaiah, as we noted in chapter 4, saw that ultimately only a person could substitute for persons. In the long run, by hindsight, Hebrews 10:4 roundly acknowledges that 'the blood of bulls and goats cannot take away sin' but the precious blood of Jesus can (Hebrews 10:12).

Progressive revelation is not a movement from error to truth, but from truth to truth, the lesser to the greater, the provisional to the permanent, the inadequate to the perfect. Indeed, 'cumulative revelation' might be a preferable term. The old view of the Bible was essentially correct when it said that the Old Testament is Jesus foreseen, the Gospels are Jesus come, the Epistles are Jesus explained and the Revelation is Jesus expected – one great, eternal, age-long, developing and climactic purpose with him as its beginning, middle and end.

God revealed

Nowhere is the description of the Old Testament as 'cumulative revelation' more exact than in its rich revelation of God himself. Even the briefest review of some divine styles and titles indicates something of this richness:

The Lord of hosts
> The LORD
> The Almighty (El Shaddai)
> The Angel of the Lord
> The Spirit of God
> The Word of God
> The Wisdom of God
The Lord is One

The Lord is many and yet one. In some ways rightly, but in most ways sadly, the NIV has allowed the literal translation 'Lord of hosts' to disappear into the interpretative words 'Lord Almighty'. The title 'Lord of hosts' (which also occurs as 'God of hosts' and 'Lord God of hosts') first appears in 1 Samuel 1:3 and after that is used over 250 times in the Old Testament. It is greatly favoured by the prophets – though, oddly, Ezekiel does not use it at all, nor does Joel. It is very likely that 'of hosts' should really be 'who is hosts'. In other words, the title does not say what the Lord possesses or has at his command but what the Lord is. In himself he is every potentiality and power. In this sense, 'Almighty' correctly reflects the meaning – 'omnipotent'.

The Name of the Lord

In order to introduce us to this veritable galaxy of powers within the divine nature, the Old Testament uses one great Name and many descriptive titles.

The one Name is 'Yahweh', represented in the NIV and most English Bibles by 'The LORD' (watch out for the capital letters as you read), but retained in The Jerusalem Bible as 'Yahweh'. This name had been known from the earliest times (Genesis 4:26) but its significance was kept secret until it was revealed to Moses (Exodus 3:13–15; 6:2–3).

Doubtless there are infinite depths in the enigmatic 'I am who/what I am' but at least we begin to sense what Exodus 3:14 is saying by noting that 'am' means 'active presence' and not just 'existence'.

In this way, to his slave people in Egypt the Lord revealed himself as essentially the 'actively present God' and his 'active presence' was seen forthwith in the exodus, the work of redeeming Israel and passing judgment on Egypt. We will discover more about this in a moment, but for now we just note that 'Yahweh' ('HE IS [actively present]') is the God who saves his people and overthrows his foes.

The God of Abraham

While sometimes calling their God 'Yahweh' (*e.g.* Genesis 16:2; 22:14), the patriarchs knew him mainly as El Shaddai (Genesis 17:1; 28:3; 35:11; 43:14; 48:3). El is a noun meaning 'God', but the meaning of 'Shaddai' is something of a mystery. The incidents where the title occurs in Genesis help us, for they reveal that El Shaddai is above all the God who comes in power into situations of human helplessness.

Powerful when humans are weakest, he makes and keeps astonishing promises so that the childless Abram becomes Abraham (Genesis 17:1,5), the father of a multitude of nations; the barren Sarah becomes a mother (Genesis 17:15); and, in due course, landless slaves possess the land of Canaan.

The Angel of the Lord

But also in Genesis we begin to meet 'the Angel of the Lord' (Genesis 16:7–14; *cf.* 31:11ff.; 48:16; Isaiah 63:8–9; *etc.*). The first passage is typical of all that follow: strangely the 'Angel' is both identified with the Lord (verse 13, *e.g.* Genesis 22:11–12) and distinguished from him (Genesis 16:11, *e.g.* Genesis 22:15,16). He possesses the divine Name (Exodus 23:21), and yet can walk with Israel when the reality of the divine presence would destroy them (Exodus 33:1–3). Not until the coming of Jesus will this enigma be solved of One who is God and yet a distinct person in his own right, who is fully divine and yet brings his divine nature down into the company of sinners.

Spirit, Word and Wisdom

The Old Testament has a doctrine of the Spirit of God parallel in every respect to that of the New Testament. A passage like Isaiah 63:11–14 indicates that the Spirit is the One who makes real the presence of God among his people, and is the agent of the blessings he designs for them. Also the Word of God (Psalm 33:6), like the Spirit (Genesis 1:2), was an agent in creation and is represented

131

as a distinct emissary of God (Psalm 107:20; Isaiah 55:11). Furthermore, in Proverbs 8:22–31 Wisdom is at least beginning to seem a distinct divine person alongside the Creator.

But in all this the Old Testament is not advertising a multiplicity of Gods. These are all just facets of the 'hosts' that comprise the divine nature. 'The Lord is one' (Deuteronomy 6:4), not in a bare, unitary sense, but as a great unity embracing an infinite multiplicity.

When they made all the mass of bits and pieces that were needed for the Tabernacle, we read that they made clasps for all the curtaining (literally) 'so that the tabernacle might become one' (Exodus 36:18), a unit (NIV) embracing a host of individual items.

Thus the Old Testament contributes to a progressive, cumulative revelation of God and it is the task of the New Testament to 'crystallize' this multiplicity into the final revelation of God the Holy Trinity. It is often thought or implied that the God revealed in the Old Testament is God the Father, while the New Testament brings in God the Son and God the Holy Spirit to complete the revelation. This is not so. The God of the Old Testament is 'the Holy Trinity incognito'. Simply with this part of the Bible available to us we would never arrive at a trinitarian doctrine of God, but the foundation for it is laid in the revelation of a God who is both simple unity and manifold diversity, 'the Lord of hosts' who is 'one Lord'.

A person giving an illustrated lecture with the help of a slide projector has to make sure that the focus is right, otherwise the pictures are all blurred round the edges. The New Testament gives the final adjustment to the Old Testament portrait of God and suddenly all is clear. The focus is now sharp. Everything in the Old Testament revelation moves into place: God is Father, Son and Holy Spirit.

God in his work: the Creator God

In what terms, then, is God revealed in the Old Testament? It begins with God, the Creator of heaven and earth.

Scientific research has much to say about heaven and earth, how they began and how they have reached their present state. Naturally there are gaps in such an account for everything is not yet known and it is all too easy to say 'Ah yes, you see, that's where God comes in' – a 'God of the gaps' view of the Creator. This is very far from what the Bible teaches.

Two sides to every story

In many circumstances we say, 'There are two sides to every story', and this is true. The weather forecaster tells us one story about our weather; it consists of high and low pressure areas, cyclones and anti-cyclones, how they are moving, when they will arrive and what the weather will consequently be like. This is the sort of thing all of us were taught at school and most of us have forgotten. But the forecaster understands all about it and, charts at hand, can show us where high or low pressures dominate – or whatever it may be.

What the forecasters cannot tell us is why it is there in the first place. And if we were to ask, they would reply, 'That's another story.' So it is with the story the Bible tells, not filling in gaps in the first story but telling the same story in another way, the story of God the Creator. The great uniformities and regularities which, for example, make weather forecasting possible (and which scientists have discovered and call 'laws') are there because he made the world to work that way.

But there is more. Science can tell us what conditions will be like in an area of high or low pressure, it cannot tell us why we are enjoying or suffering from those conditions just now. The 'why?' of it belongs with the Creator's story in which all things in heaven and earth are governed and determined by his will and serve his purposes.

The 'Creation Quadrilateral'

The truth about God the Creator goes far beyond telling a story about how things began: that, as a matter of fact, is only one side of 'the Creation Quadrilateral':

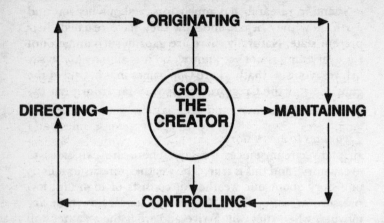

The Creator originated all things, maintains all things in existence, controls all things in operation and directs all things to their appointed destiny.

It would take up too much space to dwell on each item in this quadrilateral and to give supporting references, but it is simplicity itself to find out that this is indeed what the Old Testament says. In the Old Testament the verb 'to create' is only used with reference to God. It is never used of human works of art or craft. A concordance will tell you where to find the references to the Creator and will confirm the truth of 'the Creation Quadrilateral'.

Such a mighty view of God! So sovereign! So very much in charge of his world! Not an 'absentee landlord' but an executive managing director! It is not, of course, that the Old Testament denies the existence of 'second causes' any more than it discounts responsible human agency. We see second causes at work in the creative processes to this day in the Cheddar Caves in Somerset or Kent's Cavern in Devon, where wonders of beauty are being formed in stalactite and stalagmite by the patient agency of dripping water. But it is all under the Creator's personal hand. He is everywhere, over all, in all and through all.

God in his nature: the holy God

Psalm 145 is as rich a collection of the attributes of God as you will find in the Old Testament. It speaks of his greatness, his might and splendour (verses 3–5); his awesomeness, goodness and righteousness (verses 6–7); his grace, patience, love, and compassion (verses 8–9); his kingly glory and power (verse 11); his faithfulness and supportiveness (verses 13–14); how he provides because he loves (verses 15–17); how he is near to those who pray (verse 18); and responsive, caring and judging (verses 19–20).

What is all this about? According to verse 1 David's intention is to praise the Lord's 'name'. When, jokingly or maliciously, we give someone a 'nickname' it is to spotlight something characteristic. In the same way, the Lord's 'name' is the comprehensive summary of all his attributes, all his characteristic glories. His name is shorthand for what he has revealed about himself.

But see how the psalm ends. It has itemized all the various aspects of the Lord's name, now 'Let every creature praise his holy name for ever and ever' (verse 21). This is the supreme truth about him which sums up all the others. His name is 'holy' and he is the holy God.

What does 'holy' mean

Some say that the Hebrew word 'holiness' basically means 'separateness' or 'otherness'; others think of a base meaning of 'brightness'. In any case, as the word is used it means: (a) that God is the utterly distinct and unapproachable One; and (b) that what makes him distinct and unapproachable is his moral purity.

He belongs in a separate, distinct sphere of reality consisting of total ethical holiness. The mere idea of 'being different/belonging elsewhere' is illustrated by the fact that the woman whom Judah used as a prostitute in Genesis 38 is called (verse 21) a 'holy woman' (NIV, 'shrine-prostitute'). She was not 'holy' in any ethical sense, but she was 'separated' off to a god who was served in this way.

In the case of the God of Israel his separate distinctiveness is moral and pure: holy in its true ethical dimension. This, to put it in a word, is what makes God who he is.

God in his relationships: the covenant God

The word 'covenant' occurs for the first time in the Old Testament in Genesis 6:18, and the meaning it has there remains steady throughout the Bible.

The situation was one of world judgment. Note the sequence 'man ... man ... mankind' in Genesis 6:5,6,7. The whole human race, without exception, has sunk down in wickedness. There is nothing about humans, without exception, to give God anything but pain and grief, and a total judgment, from which none is exempt, must follow.

Covenant grace
But into this situation there comes another factor, 'grace', 'favour': Genesis 6:8, 'Noah found favour in the eyes of the Lord.' We need to be very careful here. First of all, wherever the expression occurs that 'x found favour in the eyes of y' (*cf.* Ruth 2:10), 'x' knows or thinks that there is nothing to commend him/her to 'y', nor any reason why kindness should be shown. While 'Noah found favour' is the only way in which the words can be translated, they actually mean that 'favour found Noah'.

Secondly, we must note that Genesis 6:9 marks a new beginning in the narrative. 'This is the account of Noah' is a sort of chapter heading (*cf.* Genesis 10:1). 'Account' means 'ongoing story', telling how coming events 'emerged' out of what had already happened. When we read, therefore, in Genesis 6:9 that Noah was 'righteous' etc., this is not the reason why he 'found favour' but the consequence of it. God's grace cannot be merited, but when it comes as a freely given divine gift, contrary to merit and deserving (see Genesis 6:5–7), it produces a new person.

As the Lord tells of the disaster about to overtake the

whole race, he looks back to his 'grace' relationship with Noah and says (literally) 'But I will implement my covenant with you' (Genesis 6:18). In other words, he has pledged grace to Noah and this grace will be the means of his salvation when the flood of judgment comes.

The second great covenanting in Genesis came in chapters 15 – 17 when God covenanted with Abraham.

A covenant is, of course, a promise, a freely undertaken commitment of God. The promise to Abraham is spelt out in Genesis 17:3–8. It is personal (Abram becomes Abraham, a new man with new capabilities, verses 4,5), domestic (the sort of family Abraham will have, verse 6), spiritual (God's commitment to Abraham and his children, verse 7), and territorial (the gift of Canaan, verse 8). This covenant was inaugurated on a particular day (Genesis 15:18), the day Abram prepared the covenant sacrifice which the Lord commanded (Genesis 15:9–17).

Covenant sacrifice

With Noah we learned that the covenant arose out of divine saving grace, freely given; with Abraham we learn that (somehow – for it is not explained in Genesis 15) the covenant needs to be inaugurated with a sacrifice. With Moses and the exodus, explanations and consequences both become clear, for the whole book of Exodus describes what happens when the Lord 'remembers his covenant' (Exodus 2:24), and determines to do something about it. There are two key chapters: Exodus, 12 and 24.

Passover

By the Passover sacrifice the Lord kept his people safe on the night when he entered Egypt in judgment (Exodus 12:12,13). The story is a simple one, capable of being summed up in three words. The first is *satisfaction*: when he saw the shed blood of the sacrificed lamb, the God who was bent on judgment 'passed over', for somehow that blood satisfied and allayed his wrath. Secondly, sheltering under the blood (Exodus 12:21–23), people enjoyed *safety*, without any fear that the just destroyer would touch

137

them. Thirdly, we must ask how it is that this shed blood satisfied God and shelters people. According to Exodus 12:30, 'there was not a house without someone dead'. This is a verse that speaks truer than it intended. In every Egyptian household the just judgment of God had taken the token, but dreadful form of the death of the firstborn; in the houses of Israel (Exodus 12:8–9) lay the dead body of the lamb that had been selected as sufficient to cover the number and needs of the Lord's people (Exodus 12:3–4). The lamb is thus their exact *substitute* which, in dying, delivered them, the Lord's firstborn (Exodus 4:22), from the wrath of the divine Judge. Since the lamb had died, there was no need for the Lord's firstborn to die.

At Mount Sinai

In Exodus 24:3–8 the consequent situation is enacted. The altar with its twelve surrounding pillars (verse 4) represents the Lord surrounded by his twelve-tribe people and shows them as 'rock-solid' in the presence of their God. This is what he promised to do by his redeeming work (Exodus 6:6,7) and he has done it.

But the Lord's people are only kept in his presence by the virtue of shed blood. Consequently, Moses sprinkled half the blood on the altar (Exodus 24:6). Once more, as at Passover, the first 'movement' of the blood (Exodus 12:13) is Godwards, to satisfy the 'wrath of a sin-hating God'. But now something new happens. As those whom the Lord has redeemed, the people pledge obedience and at once the remainder of the blood is sprinkled over them (Exodus 24:7,8) for, as they commit themselves to this pilgrim pathway there will be many a fall, many a shortcoming, and they will always need the blood of the lamb to keep them under the rule of grace. Then, as now, it is when we seek to walk in the light that we need and enjoy the blood of Jesus to cleanse us from all sin (1 John 1:7).

The marvellous story of this tripartite covenanting with Noah, Abraham and Moses takes nearly two whole books of the Bible to tell, but its central meaning is very, very simple: God reaches out in grace to bring undeserving people out of judgment and to himself through a substitutionary sacrifice and, by doing this, he commits them and they commit themselves to the life of obedience to his word.

**A Scenic Route Through
The Old Testament Revelation of God**

Meet the God of whom the Old Testament speaks

Four weeks of short daily Bible readings with brief notes

Week 1: God the Creator

Day 1. Read Genesis 1:1–13. Getting the place ready
The Bible insists that every bit of what we call 'reality' ('the heavens and the earth', verse 1) began with God. Nothing originated itself; he originated it all. As regards 'formless and empty', think of a sculptor sitting before a huge block of stone: at present it means nothing, but he knows how he will cut and shape it until it expresses his meaning. But of course God also created that huge block of matter to begin with! The 'Spirit of God' stands at hand ready to execute the will of God and suddenly the all-creating word is spoken. The mere expression of what God wants brings it into being! Since his workmanship is an expression of what he is himself, his first move is to fill the created universe with light.

Day 2. Read Genesis 1:14–28. Ordering life
The first three Days of God's work match the second three: Day 1, Light . . . Day 4, the ordered sequence of light, the great luminaries; Day 2, sea and sky . . . Day 5, sea and sky filled with life; Day 3, the habitable world . . . Day 6, its inhabitants. Note the verb 'to create'. The Old Testament only uses it of God: it points to things which are so great and/or so novel that they require him as their cause. Everything began with God (verse 1); animate life came from the life-giving Creator (verse 21); humankind need a threefold 'created' (verse 27), being the crown of creation and the creature *par excellence*.

Day 3. Read Psalm 33:6–11. Creator and King

Yes, it was as easy as that for the Creator – a word was enough (verses 6,9)! Think of the men and machines we need to widen a main road – what power, then, is this that simply says what is to happen! No wonder we are called to 'revere', to stand in awe (verse 8). But his power as Creator extends also into another sphere (verse 10), into the story of life on earth, history, the sphere of the plans of people and nations. Never think of the Creator simply as the One who pushed the boat out at the start and thereafter stands on the shore hoping for the best! He has the decisive word in what happens on earth, 'foiling' mankind and implementing his own will (verses 10–11). This does not mean we will understand what he is doing; it does mean we can live serenely and trustfully.

Day 4. Read Psalm 104:1–3, 10–15. 'Thy bountiful care'

It is no chance that the same-sized earth annually produces more than enough for its growing brood. The sadness is that we allow ourselves to be baffled by the challenge of distributing the Creator's bounty equitably. But what a telling, moving picture of God we have here: the wild donkey (verse 11), birds nesting and perching (verse 12), soil awaiting rainfall (verse 13), domestic beasts (verse 14), humankind (verse 15) – all alike the objects of divine, tender loving care. This has been the truth about God from the start: remember the free abundance of the Garden (Genesis 2)? His is an overflowing bounty, in the beginning unasked – laid on, waiting for the first human pair – and now, because of our sinfulness, undeserved, but still there. Bountiful care indeed!

Day 5. Read Isaiah 40:25–31. Shared strength

There are two ways of telling most stories. Astronomers can plot the heavens, describe the movement of stars, anticipate their rising and setting. Only the Bible can tell us why they are there in such reliable order – each one called by name (verse 26) and put in place by the faithful, mighty

Creator God. Never look at the night sky and think of mechanical order and necessity. Look up and worship God: He does it. And because he is limitless and un-wearying in power, everything is in place (verse 28). Learn a lesson with Isaiah: what the Creator reveals in creation he shares with us. The unfainting, unwearying God can make us like himself (verse 31).

Day 6. Read Isaiah 43:1–2. Special creation, special care

The words 'Jacob' and 'Israel' in the Old Testament do not point to someone other than you and me, they point to the Lord's people, the 'Israel of God' (Galatians 6:16), the descendants of Abraham (Romans 4:11), the 'circumcision' (Philippians 3:3). Just as the Lord created the world around us, so by the same exercise of his will and power he created us to be his people (Ephesians 2:10). And just as he superintends the world he created (see yesterday) so he lovingly superintends us, looking on us and saying, 'You are mine' (verse 1). Life is not all grim, of course, but it is in the grim days (verse 2) that we need the special assurance that he is with us and that all is well. The Lord's people are his protected species.

Day 7. Read Isaiah 65:17–25. New creation

Our sinful ways have sadly marred the beauty and proper functioning of the Lord's lovely creation. It is not enough to become 'green' and environmentally aware. We need also to lament and repent. But ultimately the Creator will not leave his workmanship to fail or languish. He will (one day, as we say) create all things anew – the environment (verse 17), people (verse 18), and experiences (verse 19). No more sadness (verse 19), no more 'curse' (verse 20; Genesis 3:14–19), no more insecurity (verse 22), but fellowship with God (verse 24) and unity throughout his created order (verse 25).

Week 2: God the revealer

Day 1. Read Exodus 3:11–15. The God who speaks

We read it so familiarly, 'The Lord said to Moses', that we can forget what a unique marvel it is that God should speak to a human being. Specially privileged people like Moses were brought into a conversational relationship with the Lord – even arguing the toss with him! But from the beginning (*e.g.* Genesis 2:16; 17:1) the Lord's people on earth have been marked off by the fact that God spoke to them, and they have the word of God to direct their lives. God has not kept silent, waiting for us to search for him. He has come out to us, telling us of himself, directing us by his word. And he kept on speaking his word until the full revelation of God was possessed on earth, our written Bibles. We are still the people of that word.

Day 2. Read Psalm 19:1–6. The hunger of natural religion

Suppose God had never spoken ... what would we know about him? The heavens do 'speak' of his glory and excite awe in us. But which voice shall we heed – the sunset telling of beauty, or the volcano telling of destruction? This is why verse 2 speaks of nature 'pouring forth knowledge' and yet verse 3 says (literally), 'There is no speech or words; their voice is not heard.' We look at nature and talk to ourselves about what we see. If that was all we had, we would remain hungry for a real, sure, unequivocal voice from heaven, a voice coming from outside ourselves, revealing to us the God we dimly sense, pulling together into one coherent revelation all the differing perceptions that come to us from the world around. Indeed we must learn to glory in what he has created – and to hunger for the sure word which, in grace to us, he has spoken.

Day 3. Read Psalm 19:7–14. The joy of knowing

Pick out the leading words: in verse 7, 'law' = 'teaching'; 'statutes' = 'testimonies' (what the Lord has 'testified' about himself); in verse 8, 'precepts' = his detailed instructions for life; 'commands' = authoritative orders; in verse 9, 'ordinances' = his royal edicts, what he has 'judged' to be right. He has not left us, you see, to fathom things out as best we can and hope to muddle through. He is a God who has spoken and his people possess his word – in our very privileged case, the complete word, the Bible. We are called to respond with our emotions (verse 10), delighting in the sweetness of his word; with mind and conscience (verses 11–13), learning, obeying, sensitive to fault; and in will (verse 14), committing ourselves to what pleases him.

Day 4. Read 1 Samuel 3:19 – 4:1. Through chosen people

The Lord's word came *to* and *through* Samuel. This simple story illustrates the Lord's way of doing things. He does not write his word in mile-high letters across the sky; he chooses people to whom and then through whom he proposes to speak. We usually call them prophets in the Old Testament and apostles in the New. Hebrews 1:1–2 outlines the process from beginning to end: the days of prophet after prophet, each of whom brought from God his own facet of divine truth, a bit here, a bit there, now by this method, now by that . . . But the whole diamond, in all its facets, shone with full brilliance only when the Son of God, our Lord Jesus Christ, came to us, validating all that had gone before, assuring us that we can trust the word of God.

Day 5. Read Psalm 119:153–160. The renewing word

For NIV 'preserve' (verses 154, 156, 159) read 'renew'. The psalmist is enduring suffering (verse 153) and foes who persecute (verse 157). His reaction is (a) to hold the Lord's law ('teaching', verse 153) in his mind; (b) to obey the Lord's statutes (what the Lord has testified about himself, verse 157) in his life; and (c) to love the Lord's precepts (his detailed requirements, verse 159) with his emotions. Life's fortunes change, but the word the Lord has spoken ('your word', verse 160) is eternal truth and an unchanging basis for living. But also the Lord who promises renewal (verse 154) and whose love guarantees that he will give us new life as we need it (verse 159) actually gives us that life as we live by his laws (verse 156, *cf.* Acts 5:32).

Day 6. Read Daniel 2:17–23. Wisdom in life's conundrums

Daniel found his God to be a God of revelation at a time of personal crisis. Reading between the lines we guess that King Nebuchadnezzar wearied of the pretensions of his 'wise men' and, when he needed an interpretation, put them deliberately on the spot by requiring them to tell both the dream and its meaning, on pain of death. Daniel banded himself with his friends into a fellowship of prayer (verses 17–18) and proved that his God is one 'who reveals' (verse 23). While we would be foolish to expect or depend upon anything as chancy as a dream, we would be equally foolish not to commit our problems to God in earnest prayer, to share our concerns with trusted friends, and to expect God to open his word to us for our guidance.

Day 7. Read Isaiah 33:17–24. The ultimate vision

The New Testament (*e.g.* Hebrews 12:22; Revelation 21:1–4) teaches us that 'Zion' (verse 20) is a picture of the heavenly blessings we now enjoy in Christ and of the future that awaits us. Here Isaiah sees it as a place of secure tenure (verse 20), unruffled peace (verse 21), the solution to all the inadequacies and failures of life (verse 23), a place of personal fulfilment and the forgiveness of sins (verse 24). But above all, the vision of the Lord the King (verse 17), ever present and saving.

Week 3: God the covenant-maker

Day 1. Read Genesis 9:8–17. A great promise made certain

In the Bible 'covenant' is used for very special promises which the Lord made. Like all 'covenant promises' this one with Noah comes on the sole initiative of God. Noah neither asked for it, nor expected it; God was not obliged to make it. He promised because he wanted to promise:

'Never again' (verses 11,15). The 'covenant sign' (verses 12,17) gives visible expression to the promise. Imagine, whenever storm clouds gathered and everything reminded him of the way the great flood had come, Noah's relief at seeing the rainbow. He would say, 'But God has promised.' Baptism and the Lord's Supper are today's covenant signs confirming to us all God's promises in Christ.

Day 2. Read Genesis 17:1–10. More promises: parents and their children

The Bible is full of the promises of God: he loves making promises. To Abram the promise was (a) personal (verse 5): he would become a new man with new powers; (b) domestic (verse 6): this is the sort of family he would have: (c) spiritual (verse 7): the Lord commits himself to Abram and his descendants; (d) territorial (verse 8), a land to live in. Next the Lord wrapped his promise up in a sign which is to be applied to Abraham, the adult believer and to his eight-day-old sons (verses 9–12). How very precious that God extends his promises to our children (Acts 2:39)!

Day 3. Read Exodus 6:1–8. God means his promises: have patience

Moses was in a deep trough of depression. He had been sent by God to bring Israel out of Egypt, but everything had gone wrong (actually through Moses' own dis-obedience and cack-handedness!). But the Lord was not knocked off course. He had made his promises long ago to Abraham and he had no intention of failing to keep them. We may fail, but he does not. What he has promised he will most certainly keep and perform. We get impatient: why has nothing happened? Why has God done nothing? But his timetable is not ours. He will keep his promises, never fear. 'Trust and Obey.' Be patient.

Day 4. Read Psalm 89:1–8. Another side to the covenant

When the Lord's people first asked him to give them a king it was indeed a lapse of real trust on their part. They

146

wanted the security of a permanent institution instead of the 'strain' of simply trusting the Lord when dangers arose. But the Lord took their second best and made it his first best, 'covenanting' to David that he would have unending kingship – and ultimately that the perfect King would reign in David's line (Luke 1:30–33). In this way God's central covenant promises came to be focused on the expected king and we know that, in fact, all God's promises have come to fulfilment in the Lord Jesus Christ (2 Corinthians 1:20). Psalm 89 is a product of a time when God did not seem to keep his promises: its message is that at such a time, far from doubting the promises, we should turn them into prayer and wait for God to keep them.

Day 5. Read Isaiah 54:5–10. The coming covenant (1). Like a true marriage: peace

The prophets took the idea of the covenant and allowed it to shape their vision of the future. Outside this covenant, life is like all the stress and trauma of a broken marriage (verse 6); or like being caught up in the great flood (verse 9). But Isaiah foresees a covenanted (*i.e.* pledged, guaranteed) peace (verse 10). The peace he speaks of is, in the first instance, peace with God, as in 53:5, secured for us by the sin-bearing work of the Lord's servant, our Lord Jesus Christ. Much of Isaiah's vision awaits fulfilment. We have peace with God (Romans 5:1) but the fruition of unbroken peace awaits the coming of Christ.

Day 6. Read Jeremiah 31:31–34. The coming covenant (2). Sin forgiven and forgotten

Jeremiah saw that the Lord would yet covenant a cluster of good things: (a) a new heart, shaped so as to obey God's law (verse 33); (b) a direct knowledge of the Lord, 'knowing' him person to person, intimately, lovingly (verse 34); and (c) all of this arising from (note 'for' at the end of verse 34) sin being forgiven and forgotten. Isaiah told us that this dealing with sin would be the work of the Lord's Servant (Isaiah 53); Jeremiah does not go into detail but leaves us to wonder at the result: the Lord has not only forgiven our sins, he has forgotten we ever committed them.

Day 7. Read Ezekiel 37:24–28. The coming covenant (3). God dwelling among his people

See how Ezekiel summarizes what Isaiah and Jeremiah said: like Jeremiah he foresaw the days of the New Covenant as marked by obedience (verse 24). Like Isaiah he foresaw a covenant of peace (verse 26). Like Psalm 89, he foresaw a coming David (verse 24). But he climaxed his vision with the thought of the Lord dwelling among his people – his perpetual and unchanging presence through an everlasting covenant promise (verse 26).

Week 4: God the Redeemer

Day 1. Read Ruth 4:1–10. The Kinsman-Redeemer

The story of Boaz and Ruth (of which we have read here only the climax: why not read the whole book?) illustrates a beautiful Old Testament provision. When people got into difficulties they could not handle – a debt, or the necessity to sell up home or land – their next-of-kin had the right to step in and make the whole burden his own, and they had the right to expect him to do so. This is what Boaz did for Naomi and Ruth: he made their difficulties his own, solved and ended them. This is one way in which, by the laws he gave them, the Lord was teaching his people to be like himself: for he is himself our next-of-kin, our Kinsman-Redeemer.

Day 2. Read Genesis 48:10–16. The Lord is like that too!

Genesis 48:16 is the first time the verb 'to redeem' (NIV 'delivered') occurs in the Bible. Jacob is approaching the end of his long, varied life. Looking back he sees one golden thread running through it all: God has been his Shepherd; the Lord's Angel (an Old Testament preview of the Lord Jesus) has been his Kinsman-Redeemer, his next-of-kin. In all his experiences and scrapes, Jacob has never been alone; there has always been a divine 'relative' identifying with him, sharing and bearing his burdens. This was the blessing Jacob sought for the sons of Joseph as he blessed them. It is our blessing too: a Shepherd to lead and care; a Kinsman-Redeemer to take upon himself every disaster that would threaten to overwhelm us.

Day 3. Read Isaiah 63:7–9. The great redemption (1). In the past

The whole passage (verses 7–14) makes it clear that Isaiah is looking back to the exodus, to the Lord's work of grace and power in bringing our ancestors out of Egyptian bondage and death. Verse 7 speaks of the Lord's 'kindness', his 'ever-unfailing love', and of his 'compassion', his heart-throbbing affection for his people – all of which led him to become their 'Saviour' (verse 8). In verse 9 we read how he identified with them in every sorrow and carried them through all their hardships in the wilderness journey. At the heart of it all is the key idea: love and pity made him their Redeemer, their next-of-kin, their divine burden-bearer.

Day 4. Read Isaiah 35:1–10. The great redemption (2). In the future

Even for Isaiah this chapter exemplifies a literary and lyrical high spot as he strains forward to see a divinely transformed people with every weakness healed (verses 5–6), in a new environment (verse 7) where every need is met. The picture of the future is drawn from the exodus of the past: a holy people on the journey home, guarded alike from their own frailty within and from every threat from outside (verses 8–9). They are on their way back to Zion (Week 2, Day 7) – and they are the Lord's 'redeemed' (verse 9). Their Kinsman-Redeemer has led them all their life through (as for Jacob, Day 2) and now he is bringing them safely home to glory.

Day 5. Read Psalm 130:1–8. Plentiful redemption

Translated in Isaiah 35:10 as 'ransom', a different word from the Kinsman-Redeemer word occurs here in verses

7 and 8. 'Ransom' is a better translation because the word focuses more on the price that has been paid (as when ransoms are paid today) than on the person (the kinsman) who does the paying. This too is part of the Lord's ever-unfailing love (verse 7). The psalm is concerned with sin (verses 1–3), in respect of which we need mercy ('grace', verse 2) and forgiveness (verse 4). But at a price. Sin cannot be overlooked or swept under the carpet. The holy law of the holy God requires a price to be paid. If he truly is our Kinsman-Redeemer we would expect him to pay it – which is exactly what he did in the Old Testament sacrifices and, finally and fully, in the Lord Jesus Christ (Hebrews 10:12).

Day 6. Read Leviticus 17:10–11. 'That will cover it'

'Blood' is very important in the Bible – for the reason given here. It is the life. We speak of 'lifeblood' because we know that loss of blood means loss of life. In this way, in the Bible, blood was the symbol of life ended in death. In verse 11 'atonement' means 'covering price': we hand over money for a debt or a purchase and we say, 'That will cover it' – *i.e.* remove it by paying for it completely. In the Old Testament, animal sacrifices 'cover', and in the New Testament, the final sacrifice of Jesus 'covers', the whole debt of our sin – removes it out of God's sight and out of God's mind by paying it in full.

Day 7. Read Isaiah 44:21–23. The blessing and joy of redemption

The Kinsman-Redeemer verb, twice in verses 22 and 23, is used in the Old Testament as a summary for all the redemption words. Our great next-of-kin takes our debt as his own and pays the price on our behalf, settling it completely. Our sins, considered as an offence to God, incurring the penalty of his law, are totally gone – as completely as a cloud or mist evaporates under the heat of the sun (verse 22). 'Offences' (verse 22) are 'rebellions', sins of the will, our deliberate refusal of the Lord and his way, our determination to have our own way. 'Sins' (verse 22) are actual, recordable wrongdoings of thought, word and deed. Thus both inwardly (in person and will) and out-wardly (in act and conduct) our sin has been dealt with – and to God's satisfaction, for he performed the work him-self as our next-of-kin.

The Cross of Christ

JOHN R W STOTT

The universal symbol of the Christian Faith is
not a crib nor a manger but a gruesome
cross. Yet many people are unclear about its
meaning, and cannot understand why Christ
had to die. In this masterly book John Stott
explains the significance of Christ's cross and
answers the objections commonly brought
against teaching on the atonement.

In the first part of the book Dr Stott shows
from the four Gospels how our Lord himself
understood the cross. In the second he argues
that 'Christ in our place' is the heart of its
meaning. Next he demonstrates what the
cross achieved and then, in the final part, he
explores what it means to live under the
cross.

Whether as superb biblical exposition, or as a
characteristically thoughtful study of
Christian belief, or as a searching call to the
church to live under the cross, John Stott's
book will have a wide appeal.

384 pages   Hardback and Large Paperback

Inter-Varsity Press

The Fight

JOHN WHITE

John White has written this book because he wants you to understand clearly what the Christian life is all about. He wants you to learn in the depths of your being that the eternal God loves you and plans only your highest good – more trust in him, more likeness to him.

But his love will bring pain as intense as your joy. For the Christian life is a fight....

"Reading *The Fight* is to inhale great draughts of fresh air into one's Christian life... This is the kind of book every 20th Century Christian should have on his book shelf."

Christian Weekly Newspapers

230 pages   Pocketbook

Inter-Varsity Press

Hear the Word
Encountering its life

JOHN WHITE, JOHN BALCHIN,
ROY CLEMENTS,
JACK KUHATSCHEK,
STEPHEN D. EYRE
Introduced by IAN COFFEY

Interpreting the Bible can easily become a dry
academic exercise. Instead, of course, it is a
means to an end – knowing the living God who
still speaks today.

In this book, John White and others share their
responses to the life and power of God's Word.
The aim is to help people to tap into its sheer
overwhelming energy. Each takes up a different
aspect of practical and effective Bible use.

There is wise and considered help on:

– how to study the Bible in all its variety
– what makes the Bible unique among the books
  of the world
– what the Bible says
– how to hear the God who speaks in Scripture
– the inspiration and authority of the Bible
– the gift of prophecy in the church today
– the dynamics of daily meeting with God and
  hearing his Word.

160 pages   *Pocketbook*

Inter-Varsity Press

Keep in Step with the Spirit

J. I. PACKER

Understanding the Spirit is a crucial task for Christian theology at all times; honouring the Spirit is a crucial task in Christian discipleship today.

Is the church in danger of overemphasizing or quenching the Spirit?
What are today's acts of the Holy Spirit?
Is charismatic life something new or unique?
Are modern spiritual gifts the same as those of the New Testament?

Dr Packer considers these questions in the light of Scripture and Christian history, and issues a radical challenge to personal and corporate revival.

'. . . this is a helpful, timely book which has much to teach the Church today.'

Christian Weekly Newspapers

302 pages   Large paperback

Inter-Varsity Press

Know the truth

BRUCE MILNE

'You will know the truth,' said Jesus, 'and the truth will set you free.'

Christians have already begun to know God and his truth. This handbook will help us to grow in that liberating knowledge, as it opens up the great themes of God's Word and shows us how they fit together.

Each chapter looks at one facet of biblical truth and encourages further study with Scripture references to look up, questions for discussion and books for additional reading. The main sections all close with practical reflection on how the Bible's teaching challenges us and moves us to adore the living God.

288 pages   Large paperback

Inter-Varsity Press

The Prophecy of Isaiah

ALEC MOTYER

Traditionally known as 'the evangelical prophet',
with whole passages made familiar by Handel's
Messiah, the book of Isaiah requires a commentator
of rare spiritual insight if justice is to be done to its
magnificent oracles. In Alec Motyer such a person
has been found.

He sees the book as a mosaic made up of prophesies
with different points of origin and individual
pre-histories. These are brought into an overall
unity by the prophet whose name it bears.
Unconventionally, he regards the prophecy as
consisting of three books: that of the King (1-37),
the Servant (38-55), and the Anointed Conqueror (56-66).
The three make a single picture in which each needs
the other.

Although this long awaited commentary is based on
the New International Version, the author often
supplies his own, more literal, translation, in order to
bring out the meaning of the text more exactly. His aim
throughout is to interpret the pieces of the mosaic in
relation to the book of Isaiah as a whole.

554 pages   Hardback

Inter-Varsity Press

Too Busy Not To Pray
Slowing down to be with God
BILL HYBELS

"For many years", confesses Bill Hybels, "I knew more about prayer than I ever practised."

Does that sound familiar? Most of us feel a niggling guilt at not 'praying enough'. Prayer takes time and stillness – and we're so busy!

Bill Hybels found a way out, "I did something absolutely radical," he says, "I prayed."

Now he shares what prompted him to take that life-changing step, and how you too can embark on the same adventure.

Bill Hybels is Senior Pastor of Willow Creek Community Church, South Barrington, Illinois.

160 pages   *Pocketbook*

Inter-Varsity Press